Reluctant Hero

The Story of Eastern Airlines Flight 1320

Robert M. Wilbur III

Copyright 2019 - Robert M. Wilbur III

All rights reserved. No part of this book may be reproduced or transmitted in any form or by any means, electronic or mechanical including photocopying, recording or by any information storage and retrieval without the expressed written permission of the publisher

ISBN: 9781090674814

Independently published by Robert M. Wilbur III

Dedication

This book is dedicated first and foremost to First Officer James E. Hartley, Jr. who sacrificed everything for his passengers and fellow crew members on the night of March 17, 1970. And to my father, Captain Robert M. Wilbur, Jr., who's unrivaled skill turned an impossible situation into an amazing story of survival. Their bravery speaks for itself. In their honor, and out of respect for the incredible events which took place that night, this book is not, "Based on a true story," or, "Inspired by real events." It IS the true and unfiltered story of the hijacking of Eastern Airlines Flight 1320.

"Courage is grace under pressure"----Ernest Hemingway

"Courage and perseverance have a magical talisman before which difficulties disappear and obstacles vanish into air."----John Quincy Adams

"I wanted you to see what real courage is . . . It's when you know you're licked before you begin, but you begin anyway and see it through no matter what."----Harper Lee, *To Kill a Mockingbird*

Contents

Prologue

1 Flight 1320

2 Aviation Security: A Brief History

3 Captain Robert M. Wilbur, Jr.

4 First Officer James E. Hartley, Jr.

5 John Joseph Divivo, Jr.

6 The Flight Attendants

7 The Hijacking

8 On the Ground

9 The Prosecution

10 Time to Heal

11 Back in Boston

12 The Reluctant Hero

13 Life Goes On

14 Like Father Like Son?

15 The End of an Era

16 Finishing What He Started

17   Reconnecting with the Hartleys

Epilogue

Acknowledgments

Bibliography

Pictures and More

Prologue

I was just two and a half years old when my father became a hero. His story is, by miles, the most impressive and awe-inspiring account of heroism perpetrated by two men that I've ever heard. But almost more incredible than the act itself is just how little known the story of Eastern Airlines Flight 1320 is. Like most of us I don't have a real acute recollection of people or events long past. There are times I wish I was more like Marilu Henner. You remember her from the show *Taxi*. She has something called Highly Superior Autobiographical Memory, or H-SAM. Give her any date from ten, twenty, even thirty years ago, and she can recall to the smallest detail, where she was, who she was with, and everything she did that day. My short-term memory is just fine, and like most people, the extent of my recollections of events in the distant past are an unreliable assortment of bits and pieces of out-of-context information. These shadowy images never seem to be enough and I'm almost always left wanting more. But whenever any of us wish we had total recall of things in our past, like Marilu, it's important to remember that such a gift would come at a heavy price. We wouldn't be able to choose only to have clear recollections of the good things and, therefore, our traumatic memories would have all the more power to inflict pain.

Some of my most vivid memories from long ago involve walking through the airport with my father. He was a pilot for Eastern Airlines, Captain Robert M. Wilbur, Jr., and as such, he and his family enjoyed the unique benefit of flying for free. Like the families of most commercial pilots, we took advantage of that perk, usually taking a trip or two every year. As a teenager in the 1980s, I remember the thrill of him sneaking me into Eastern's flight simulator a time or two. The experience of walking through the airport with him as a child, and early teen, is solidly burned into my memory, as few other things are. Now, I've never walked side by side with an A List celebrity, but I imagine the feeling must be similar, minus all the paparazzi and autograph seekers of course. When I walked the airport with my father it was more the looks he got, and the way he was treated, not only by Eastern Airlines employees, but by just about everyone who worked in the industry. Pilots in uniform always garner some attention at airports. People admire the skill it must take to fly a big airplane, the exotic travel, the adventure. It's one of those really cool jobs, and the look is pretty cool too. But this was much more than that. He was treated like royalty, like a movie star, only different. There was this undercurrent of real admiration and respect. When you're a kid, your dad is just your dad, but whenever we walked with him through an airport, especially in the New York area, I realized that my dad was something more.

It's hard to believe, but the incident that made our father famous, if only within the airline industry, was almost never discussed in our home. So unexplored, and generally unwelcome, was the topic of our father's incident, that it eventually faded comfortably into the background. It wasn't that it was forgotten, not by family, or friends, or by people in the industry. Over time, however, it atrophied, shrunk, somehow became so much less than it was. Great events always fade over time, but the incredible story of the hijacking of Eastern Airlines Flight 1320 disappeared from memory far too quickly. However unjust that might seem to the rest of us, it was more than okay with the modest hero who was at the controls of the airplane that night. The antithesis of an aggrandizing self-promoter, when the 1970's version of a media blitz made its run at him, my father eschewed the limelight, ran from the cameras, and deflected credit to others. A recording of the communications between Boston air traffic control and the two pilots of Flight 1320 that night has been in our family's possession since 1970, yet my sister, Allison, and I, listened to the recording for the very first time on January 31, 2016. It brought us both to tears. Allison has a master's degree in special education, with a specialty in applied behavioral analysis, from Colombia University, in other words, she's pretty bright, and knows a thing or two about behavior. She's always felt that, in addition to living with the remnants of post-traumatic stress, our father still suffers from survivor guilt even after all these years.

On the very rare occasion when my sister and I cornered our father and pressed him on the subject, he would offer few details, and would quickly change the subject with an expertise honed over time. We both recall small dinner gatherings at our house in the 1970s with some of my father's pilot friends in attendance. In addition to the sports, politics, and events-of-the-day chit-chat required at any such gathering, the group would usually talk about work, and as pilots, they talked about flying. Now you can imagine that it wouldn't take very long for the subject of my father's hijacking to take center stage. His pilot friends would laugh and say things like, "He turned on the No Smoking sign and the Fasten Seatbelt sign." "Bob, how did you ever follow the checklist in a situation like that?" "Why didn't you tell anyone that you were shot?" My dad would always smile with them, and offer very little, if anything, by way of an explanation. Before employing his efforts to change the subject, he would always give credit to his first officer, James E. Hartley, Jr., who gave his life to save the other seventy-two passengers and crew aboard Flight 1320.

1. Flight 1320

Tuesday, March 17, 1970, started out as any other day might start in the Wilbur household. Dad always had coffee and read the *Bergen Record* from cover to cover, and this day was no different. My mother, Anita, took care of her two-and-a-half-year-old son (me), while Dad dropped my four-year-old sister, Allison, off at nursery school. My maternal grandmother Mary Decicco, affectionately known to the family as GaGa, was also at our house that day, visiting from Scranton, Pennsylvania. This would, of course, turn out to be fortuitous timing for a visit given what was to take place later that night. GaGa would be called upon to babysit my sister and me for a rather extended period.

Dad had been with Eastern Airlines since 1959 but had only recently been promoted to captain. He'd been on the DC-9-31 for approximately three months, including training, but was already very comfortable with the airplane, and he had flown the shuttle routes from the New York/New Jersey area to Boston and Washington repeatedly over the previous two months.

According to the National Weather Service, there were clear skies and a high temperature of 46 degrees on March 17, 1970. Surface winds at Newark Airport were out of the west/southwest at 11 mph, and there was 13 miles of visibility. The weather in Boston was much the same that day. Not exactly stressful conditions for a seasoned pilot flying a short and familiar route.

The day's work was to entail two round-trip flights from Newark, New Jersey, to Boston, Massachusetts. The first leg of the trip, Flight 1280, was scheduled to depart Newark Airport at 3:30 p.m. My father says that he probably left our home on Berdan

Avenue in Fair Lawn, New Jersey, at around 1:45 p.m. in order to arrive a bit early for his 2:30 p.m. check-in. My mom specifically remembers kissing my dad goodbye before he left for the airport that day.

After arriving at work, Captain Wilbur went through his usual routine of reporting to Flight Operations to begin his pre-flight. He looked over the dispatch release, which includes weather reports, estimated load, and suggested fuel. The shuttle flight's load could only be estimated because passengers didn't pre-book tickets, they simply showed up, and paid their fare in cash after boarding. After the captain and the dispatcher agreed on fuel, paperwork was signed, and the flight plan was finalized. It was First Officer James Hartley's job to perform a physical inspection of the airplane, a walk-around, which he did.

"Before the first leg of the trip, Jim had asked the crew if anyone had a stamp. He wanted to get a letter out to his kids before leaving Newark," flight attendant Arlene Albino recalled. "I happened to have one in my bag, and I gave it to him. He handed me a dime, which was the cost of a stamp back then, insisting that I take it. I remember him saying, 'no take it, a penny saved is a penny earned.'"

Flight 1280 went off without a hitch, leaving on time, and arriving at Logan International Airport in Boston only fifty minutes after takeoff. Jim Hartley handled both the takeoff and landing on this first leg of the four-leg trip. The captain was tasked with flying legs two and three, with Jim handling the fourth leg, which, as it turns out, would never be flown.

Airline pilots are at their busiest during and shortly after takeoff, and then again on approach and landing. The beginning and the end of flights. It makes perfect sense.

Those are the times when air traffic is most congested. Planes are either all leaving the same place or all arriving at the same place, and they're closer to the ground, making any mechanical failure more dangerous. In addition, pilots, especially those flying in and out of airports in heavily populated urban areas, must pay strict attention to noise abatement rules. During takeoff and climb-out, departure control is contacted, radar contact established, and a specific heading must be flown. Likewise, during approach to landing, commercial pilots typically contact approach control, establish radar contact, and are given a specific heading and altitude to maintain. Approach control makes pilots aware of other traffic, but the pilots themselves are ultimately responsible for the safety of their passengers and crew and must be vigilant in avoiding other aircraft. Approach control eventually sequences all arriving aircraft for landing. One pilot does the flying, while the other handles radio communications, and both keep a keen eye on the sky.

The in-between times give pilots a bit of a break to relax and talk. My dad can't recall all these years later exactly what he and his first officer talked about that day. He'd flown with Jim, who began his career with Eastern in 1966, numerous times just in the previous two weeks, but they had only recently gotten together socially. Three days prior to the infamous flight, on a Saturday night, Jim and his wife, Becky Hartley, came over to our house to play Bridge with my parents. My dad says they spoke about the possibility of getting together again the following weekend. He liked Jim a lot and, in addition to their shared passion for flying, they had a lot in common. Jim had served in the army and my father was ex–air force, and they often talked about their days in the military. Both men were born and raised in Florida, were huge sports fans, and loved to play cards and enjoy a libation when the occasion called for it. My dad already considered Jim a friend, and my mom thought he and Becky were nice, down to earth people, whom she wanted to get to know better. A bourgeoning friendship between the Wilburs and the Hartleys may have been in the offing but, sadly, it wasn't to be. Jim Hartley was certainly more than just a friend to my dad on that St. Patrick's Day night so long ago.

The same work-horse DC-9-31 was used in all legs of the trip. The plane's flight number was changed and pre-flight was performed in operations for each leg. The smoke-filled rooms that housed flight operations in those days also contained within them a crew lounge where flight crews could relax a bit and unwind before and after trips. Given the rather routine nature of air travel, work related talk didn't need to dominate the conversation, and flight crews got to know each other a bit.

Flight 1301 departed Logan at approximately 5:30 p.m. for its return trip to Newark, New Jersey. It was, again, smooth sailing, this time with the captain handling the flying, and his co-pilot working the radio. Pre-flight procedures for the third leg of the trip were the same as before. Flight 1320 was pushed away from the gate in Newark at approximately 7:30 p.m., engines were started, and ground control cleared the plane to taxi to runway 22R. There was a total of seventy-three souls on board including; sixty-eight passengers, Senior Flight Attendant Christine Dorothy Peterson, flight attendants Arlene Florence Albino and Sandra Kay Saltzer, First Officer James E. Hartley, Jr., and Captain Robert M. Wilbur, Jr. An altimeter setting was obtained, either from Newark ground control while taxiing, or from the latest weather sequence in the pilots' possession, my father can't quite recall. The captain taxied his aircraft into position on runway 22R and was given takeoff clearance following a minimal delay.

After takeoff and climb to 2,000 feet, the flight turned right to a heading of 330° to intercept the LaGuardia VORTAC (very high frequency omnidirectional range collocated tactical air—basically a navigation aide). Newark departure control cleared step altitude changes up to 11,000 feet. Shortly after intercepting and following the 070° radial from the LaGuardia VORTAC, the flight was cleared to its cruising altitude of 17,000 feet. Flight 1320 was proceeding by the numbers in calm, clear weather conditions, and was now heading east/northeast directly toward Boston. It was at this time that the Fasten Seatbelt sign was turned off, and the flight attendants began walking the aisles collecting the $21 fare from passengers. The $21 one-way fare from Newark to Boston in 1970 equates to about $106 today. Flight attendants rotate their duties on multi-leg trips much the same way pilots do. Christine Peterson and Sandy Saltzer were charged with collecting fares on Flight 1320.

When the flight reached the Madison, Connecticut VORTAC, First Officer Hartley, who was handling radio communications, was directed to change from Newark departure control's frequency to Boston approach control. Updated altimeter settings were given along the way, and shortly after passing the Norwich, Connecticut VORTAC, Boston control gave clearance for a descent to 5,000 feet. At approximately 8:00 p.m. the short flight was between 25 and 30 nautical miles south/southwest of Logan Airport, and nearing its destination. It was at this point that Flight Attendant Sandy Saltzer rang the cockpit informing the captain that one of the passengers wanted to see him. As I stated previously, pilots have a great deal to do during their approach to landing, and they have to be doubly alert at this stage of the flight. The captain told Sandy they were far too busy, and that they wouldn't be able to see anyone until the plane was on the ground. In as cool a voice as she could muster under the circumstances, Sandy replied, "You don't understand, Captain. He has a gun!"

2. Aviation Security: A Brief History

A glimpse into the history of commercial aviation security and a look at some of its more egregious incidents, will help to paint a clearer picture of how an individual could so easily carry a loaded weapon aboard a commercial airliner in the year 1970.

On November 1, 1955, United Airlines Flight 629, a Douglas DC-6, departed Denver, Colorado, bound for Portland, Oregon. It exploded shortly after takeoff killing every one of the thirty-nine passengers and five crew members on board. Investigators found that a man named Jack Gilbert .Graham had planted a bomb in his mother's luggage with the hope of cashing in on her life insurance policy. The incident is among the first, and most deadly, criminal acts committed against a domestic airliner. Graham was convicted of multiple counts of murder and eventually executed.

On January 6, 1960, National Airlines Flight 2511 departed Idlewild Airport in New York (now JFK) bound for Miami, Florida. The plane exploded in mid-air killing all thirty-four people on board, twenty-nine passengers and five crew. The Civil Aeronautics Board investigation never made a concrete finding but suspected that a suicidal passenger had smuggled a bomb on board. The investigation lies dormant but remains open to this day.

On May 1, 1961, National Airlines Flight 337 from Miami to Key West was hijacked by a man named Antulio Ramirez Ortiz. Armed with only a steak knife, which he held to the captain's throat, Ortiz demanded to be taken to Havana, Cuba. Ortiz spun a wild and barely coherent tale about needing to warn Fidel Castro about an assassination plot against him. The crew, as they had been trained, did not resist, and the flight was diverted to Cuba. It was the very first hijacking of a U.S. passenger aircraft, and it certainly confused the hell out of Cuban air traffic controllers, who initially threatened to blow the plane out of the sky, before allowing it to land at a military base outside of Havana. Ortiz was granted asylum by the Cuban government. This event, unfortunately, turned out to be a precursor to what would become a dangerous trend. From 1968 to 1973 there were roughly sixty-nine successful hijackings to Cuba. More than half of the hijackers were fugitives seeking refuge in a country with no extradition treaty with the United States. By early 1970, Eastern Airlines had the dubious distinction of being the most hijacked airline in the world. Ten Eastern flights were hijacked in 1969 alone, nearly all to Cuba. Geographically, Eastern had a bit of an unfair advantage in this regard. Its hub and base of operations, was located in Miami, only ninety short miles from Cuba.

In 1969 the Federal Aviation Administration developed a hijacker psychological profile as well as hand-held metal detectors to screen both passengers and bags. Unfortunately only those individuals who exhibited "suspicious" behavior would be screened, and this amounted to only 0.5 percent of all commercial passengers. Ironically, Eastern Airlines was among the first to begin using metal detectors in 1969. Other airlines would follow suit on a limited basis, but there was still no law or FAA regulation mandating the use of metal detectors. Long-time family friend and retired Eastern Airlines Captain, J.P. Tristani, recently conveyed an interesting anecdote which underscores just how prevalent weapons aboard aircraft were circa 1970. He said that pilots would occasionally ask gate agents to make an announcement indicating that passengers would be searched prior to boarding. This type of announcement would invariably produce any number of guns and knives to be left in pots, planters, and garbage cans in the pre-boarding area. Pilots certainly voiced their concerns, and the evidence of the extent of the problem was overwhelming. Many more incidents would follow.

On the afternoon of November 24, 1971, a man identifying himself as Dan Cooper approached the counter of Northwest Orient Airlines in Portland, Oregon, and bought a one-way ticket on Flight 305, bound for Seattle, Washington. He paid cash for his ticket and strolled onboard the 727, briefcase in hand. "Dan" sat in his seat and ordered a bourbon and soda while waiting for the plane to take off. Shortly after departure he handed one of the flight attendants a note which indicated that he was carrying a bomb in his briefcase and asked her to sit with him. The stunned stewardess did as she was told. Cooper proceeded to crack open his briefcase giving the stewardess a glimpse of its contents. He showed her a mass of wires and red colored sticks resembling dynamite and forced her to write a note which she was to bring to the captain. The note demanded that the captain arrange an exchange with authorities once they were on the ground.

When the plane landed in Seattle, the hijacker exchanged the flight's thirty-six passengers for $200,000 and four parachutes. "Cooper" kept several crew members onboard including, of course, the pilots. The hijacker demanded that the plane take off and set course for Mexico City, at an altitude of no more than 10,000 feet. At just past 8:00 p.m. local time, somewhere between Seattle and Reno, "Dan Cooper" did the unthinkable. He donned one of the parachutes and jumped out of the back of the plane into the frigid night with the $200,000 strapped to his body. The pilots landed safely, but the man who called himself Dan Cooper was never seen or heard from again.

Thus began one of the great unsolved mysteries in American law enforcement history. The FBI interviewed hundreds of suspects over the years but never made an arrest. In 1980 a young boy found a rotting package filled with $5,800 in twenty-dollar bills along the Columbia River. The bills matched the ransom money serial numbers, but whatever became of "Dan Cooper" himself or the rest of the money remains a mystery to this day. In 2016, some forty-five years after the hijacking, the FBI finally closed its active investigation. The D.B. Cooper case, as it was dubbed by the media, spawned a few books, TV shows, and movies, and sparked the interest of the American public to a degree rivaled by few other things of like stature or importance. But what it obviously did not have the power to do was to change the overall mindset of the airline industry.

On October 25, 1972, Charles A. Tuller, a self-proclaimed "White middle-class revolutionary," and his two sons, Bryce, age nineteen, and Jonathan, age seventeen, along with their seventeen-year-old friend, William White Graham, attempted to rob the Crystal City Bank in Arlington, Virginia. During the failed robbery, police officer Israel Gonzales and bank manager Harry J. Candee were shot and killed. The group fled to Houston, Texas, where, on October 29, 1972, the four gunmen shot their way on to an Eastern Airlines flight, killing an Eastern ticket agent and wounding a maintenance worker in the process. Not surprisingly, they demanded to be taken to Cuba.

Although they were never extradited, the Tullers and Graham found life in Cuba "a living hell," and they found their way back to America in 1975. That same year, Bryce Tuller attempted to rob a Kmart in Fayetteville, North Carolina, and was arrested. Charles and youngest son Jonathan turned themselves in four days later. William White Graham, however, remained at large until 1993. He surrendered to authorities after seeing himself featured on an episode of America's Most Wanted.

In December 1972, the FAA issued an emergency mandate requiring *all* passengers and carry-on bags to be either screened by metal detectors or searched by hand. The FAA ruling also required airports to station armed security guards at boarding checkpoints. Congress enacted the 1974 Air Transportation Security Act, officially sanctioning the FAA screening rule, which was already being carried out in earnest by late 1973. By the mid-1970s, at least one hundred and fifty planes had been "Skyjacked" in the United States alone, and radical groups in the Middle East had turned to hijackings as a way to seize the spotlight and further their own political agendas.

Increased terrorist activity in the mid-1980s cut deeply into the revenues of nearly every international carrier. Passengers were afraid, and they were staying home in droves. Business on a number of Pan-American Airlines international routes, for example, had fallen by as much as 50 percent. In an effort to reassure passengers and assuage fear, and thereby increase profits, Pan-Am established its own security operation in 1986. They formed a company, Alert Management Systems, Inc., and placed a man at the helm who had no particular expertise in the business of security. Fred Ford, Alert Management's first president, had been vice president of Pan Am's general aviation division and was simply reassigned to run the new company. The cost of the additional security was funded, in part, by a five-dollar surcharge added to the price of every international ticket. But what were passengers really paying for?

The security measures rolled out by Pan Am were under no government mandate or oversight, and were, by any reasonable analysis, cosmetic in nature. For example, when Alert Management Systems began operating at New York's JFK Airport, they paraded German Shepherds in front of Pan Am passengers at check-in. A passenger boarding an international flight on a Pan Am aircraft would likely assume that all the checked baggage on his or her plane had been vetted by bomb sniffing dogs. The problem was, the dogs were just dogs, with no special skills or training. The frontline security personnel, likewise, seemed devoid of any special skills or training. A perfect example of this was Alert Management employee Sabine Fuches. During an investigation of the company's personnel, Ms. Fuches admitted having no background or training in security whatsoever yet was employed as a screener who interviewed passengers in an effort to determine if they might be carrying weapons or explosives on board Pan Am aircraft. She previously worked as a hairdresser.

Pan Am went further still, publicizing the fact that they had contracted with Ktalav Promotion and Investment Ltd., a security consulting firm, to review security operations at more than two dozen airports. A confidential report submitted to Pan Am officials by Ktalav Promotions offered up a scathing review of Pan Am's security measures, but it was an in-house report which was ultimately buried. When Fred Ford woke up and began to complain about inadequate airport security, he was dismissed as president of Alert Management, and returned to his post in the general aviation division.

On December 21, 1988, at 6:00 p.m. local time, Pan American Airlines Flight 103 pushed away from the jetway of the newly renovated Terminal #3 at Heathrow Airport in London, England. The 740,000-pound Boeing 747 Jumbo Jet was carrying 259 men, women, and children: 243 passengers and sixteen crew members. There were 189 Americans on board, including 38 Syracuse University students returning home to their families after a semester of study in London. After a delay of approximately twenty-five minutes on the taxi-way awaiting his turn behind other aircraft at the always busy Heathrow Airport, Captain James MacQuarrie was cleared for takeoff on runway 27L. The huge jet with its precious cargo was bound for New York's Kennedy International Airport, but the routing of the westbound transatlantic flight would first take it north, over Scottish airspace.

At 6:58 p.m., Flight 103 had reached its cruising altitude of 31,000 feet and was on a heading of 321° when it made contact with Scottish air traffic controllers. At approximately 7:02 p.m. the plane vanished from radar, and all radio communication was lost. An explosion in the front cargo hold had punched a twenty-inch hole in the fuselage effectively blowing off the nose of the aircraft. According to FAA and British Department for Transportation investigators, the plane's nose hung by a thread of metal for roughly three seconds before shearing off and smashing into Engine #3. Flight 103 went on a rapid descent to 19,000 feet before its dive became nearly vertical. The aircraft's attitude and unnatural airspeed caused it to break apart, and its wings, containing 200,000 pounds of jet fuel, dislodged as it plummeted toward the sleepy town of Lockerbie, Scotland. The wreckage of the plane was scattered over a radius of nearly two miles. The enormous weight of falling debris, along with the accompanying fireball caused by ignited jet fuel, destroyed much of the town, killing eleven people on the ground, along with every one of the 259 passengers and crew aboard the aircraft.

The subsequent three-year investigation was the largest multi-jurisdictional undertaking up to that point in history. In the end it was determined that a small but powerful symtex explosive, placed within a radio cassette recorder, was smuggled aboard the aircraft in a piece of Samsonite luggage. Flight 103 had originated in Frankfurt, Germany, as a Boeing 727, with 125 passengers on board, most of whom would take the connecting 747 from London to New York. Pan Am's records showed only seventy checked bags on the flight, out of which only a small fraction had been closely examined. Investigators learned that security personnel in Frankfurt had x-rayed a total of ten suitcases, three garment bags, and one box. What of the others? The buried report submitted to Pan Am officials by Ktalav Promotions is eerily prophetic. Security officer Isaac Yeffet is quoted as saying, "Pan Am is highly vulnerable to most forms of terrorist attack"… "a bomb would have a good chance of getting through security at the Frankfurt Airport"… "The fact that no major disaster has occurred to date is merely providential," and last but not least, "It appears, therefore, that Pan Am is almost totally vulnerable to a mid-air explosion.…" Following the crash of Pan American Flight 103 over Lockerbie, Scotland, U.S. carriers at European and Middle Eastern airports began mandating that all checked baggage be x-rayed, and that all bags be matched with a passenger on board. It is important to make clear that these were self-imposed rules, carried out by the airlines themselves at their own expense. Despite the tragic death of 270 people, 189 of whom were American citizens, neither the FAA nor any other government agency imposed additional security mandates. In 1988, Pan Am Flight 103 was the deadliest terrorist attack against the United States in history. Throughout the 1990s the Government Accountability Office (GAO), the auditing and investigative arm of the United States Congress, offered up warning after warning regarding the sub-par state of aviation security.

Incredibly, as late as the year 2000, only international flights from U.S. airports were subject to checked baggage security measures. Could it be that up to that point in aviation history there was insufficient loss of life to move the airline industry, the FAA, or any number of other government regulators or lawmakers to act in a more meaningful way? How many deaths would it take?

The answer to that question came on September 11, 2001, and anyone who flies these days understands that the pendulum has swung 180 degrees in the other direction. Today we wait in long security lines, take off our belts and shoes, subject ourselves and our children to x-ray scanning and random pat down searches. All our luggage, carry-on bags, and possessions are scanned for potential weapons and explosives.

My father was interviewed six days after the September 11, 2001, hijackings. On September 17, 2001, NBC's *Dateline* sent a crew to his house in Florida to get his impressions on a number of topics, including steel cockpit doors and whether or not pilots should carry firearms on board their aircraft. It might surprise people, especially given the ordeal he went through some thirty-one years prior, but to the latter question his answer was an emphatic NO. My father has always felt that vital security measures have to be taken on the ground.

This very abridged overview of the history of aviation security is not all-encompassing and is not meant to be an indictment of the airline industry. As with all things, hindsight is 20-20, and concern for individual liberty should always be of paramount importance in a free society. Although in looking back, one can't help but be surprised, especially given the available technology, at how very slow the industry moved to put appropriate security measures in place to safeguard its employees and passengers. This look back should certainly make one thing abundantly clear to the reader. In 1970 an individual could bring a loaded gun aboard a commercial plane as easily as he or she might bring one aboard a city bus.

3. Captain Robert M. Wilbur, Jr.

My father worked a lot and was a great provider for our family. By word and example, he taught my sister and me important lessons about honesty, integrity, and responsibility. Growing up in a military family, and having served in the military himself, he lived those values, and they seemed to come as easily to him as breathing. When he wasn't away on trips, he made every effort to spend time with us. He went outside and played catch with me, coached some of my little league teams, and played tennis with my sister Allison and me. He played Monopoly with us, took us to amusement parks, the movies, out to dinner, and took our family on vacation. I'm sure that in addition to fulfilling his responsibilities as a father, which was very important to him, he honestly enjoyed it.

Not having grown up in a terribly warm or nurturing environment, my dad struggled with some of the other aspects of fatherhood. He wasn't the type to sit at our bedsides and stroke our hair after a particularly bad day or a bad dream had moved us to tears. When life revealed its sometimes harsh and unfair nature, he wouldn't sit us on his lap and tell us everything would be alright. He didn't listen intently to our childish hopes and dreams. I don't remember any long conversations with my dad about the meaning of life, and I can't remember ever seeing him cry, although my mom told my sister and me that he cried like a baby when his mother died in 1979. I guess it could be that, for whatever reason, he wanted to keep the softer side of himself from his children, but I kind of doubt that. As much as our father lacked the ability or willingness to demonstrate a softer side, our Italian mother picked up the slack. She listened and stroked and cared and talked, and then listened some more. She still does to this day. They say opposites attract, and my parents are a case in point. They've been happily married since 1965.

My dad didn't sit around the kitchen table and listen to his children's accounts of their day. At best he would drift in and out of the room picking up little pieces of out of context information. He would sometimes ask way off-the-mark questions based on these snippets of information he overheard, usually prompting my mom, my sister, and I, to laugh hysterically. My mom would sometimes become exasperated after repeated instances of this and admonish him for paying so little attention.

High school years always seem to be accompanied by lots and lots of drama, and our house was no exception. While I was certainly not immune, and at the risk of throwing her under the bus, my sister, Allison, brought home the lion's share. Now, I'll be the first to admit that it's not particularly interesting, and sometime quite painful, to listen to the constant he said/she said, who's going to the dance with whom, "I hate her, she's not my friend anymore," boyfriend/girlfriend drama of a high school girl. However, the conversations between my mother and sister on these topics were so ongoing, and so often repeated, that anyone living with them would have no choice but to become familiar with the cast of characters discussed. Anyone that is, except our father. He would invariably enter a room with my mom, my sister, and sometimes me, in mid-conversation about an already beaten to death topic and ask the dreaded, "WHO," question. "Who said that?" "Who did that?" "Who are you talking about?" This too generated lots of laughs, and one of us, usually Mom, would say something like, "Who- who the owl, if you really wanna know what's going on, sit down and listen!"

My father is the type of man who never overhypes his own accomplishments while excusing away failures or shortcomings. He is all substance without the fluff. He projects, in both his words and actions, an attitude which says, in no uncertain terms, get the job done, and there really isn't any excuse good enough. Yet, more often than not, he is able to do so without sounding like a drill sergeant. My dad can be very engaging when the mood strikes him. Even at eighty-four years old, he has a sharp mind, a quick wit, and a playful sense of humor.

To try to characterize my dad as cold or distant would, no doubt, be unfair. He loves all of us and demonstrates that love in his own way. However, I don't think it would be terribly inaccurate to describe him as a bit of a loner, and certainly emotionally detached to a certain degree. I truly believe that this cool, unemotional demeanor, inherent in my father, played a key role in the survival of Eastern Airlines Flight 1320. But as is usually the case, in order to better understand the nature of a man, we have to go back to the beginning, back to where he came from.

***

Robert Milton Wilbur, Jr. was born on March 30, 1934, in Lakeland, Florida, to parents Robert Milton Wilbur, Sr. and Elsie Freeman Greene Wilbur. He grew up in relative privilege due, in no small part, to the wealth of his maternal grandparents. Henry Francis Greene was born in Montreal Canada to English parents. During his early formative years he was sent to live with relatives in England where he attended school before returning to America. Henry graduated from Cooper Union College in New York's East Village with a degree in Engineering. While in school, he met and began dating my great grandmother, Charlotte Boast Greene, who lived in Bayonne, New Jersey. The two courted for a time and married shortly after Henry's graduation.

With job prospects in the engineering field seen as less than ideal to him in the Northeast, Henry looked for career prospects elsewhere. After weighing his options, Henry decided that he and Charlotte would relocate south, where he saw a golden opportunity to catch on with a large, reputable firm. Henry was able to secure a job with the Coronet Phosphate Company in Plant City, Florida. He was highly intelligent and very good at his trade, and quickly move up the ranks, eventually becoming the companies' general manager. H. F. Greene, as he would later be called (I think you have to achieve a certain level of financial success before you're allowed to turn your first name into an initial), bought stock very early on in the Coronet Phosphate Company, and did quite well. He was a strong willed, rather forceful and, at times, gruff individual, who never lacked for self-confidence, and he demanded as much of others as he did of himself. My great grandmother, Charlotte, in contrast, was a soft spoken and mild-mannered woman, who presented as far more diminutive than her somewhat ample frame might suggest. Henry and Charlotte lived in the manager's house on the grounds of Coronet. They would eventually have four children: three sons, Ernest, Harry and Brower, and finally, their youngest, Elsie, my grandmother.

The Wilbur clan hailed from Missouri, and for reasons unexplained by those who keep our family history, they relocated to Plant City, Florida, circa early 1920s. My grandfather, Robert M. Wilbur, Sr., graduated from Plant City High School in just three years. He attended the United States Naval Academy in Annapolis, Maryland, graduating in 1932 with a degree in mechanical engineering. Apparently not thrilled with the prospect of lengthy deployments out on the high seas cooped up with hundreds of other men, he resigned his commission and returned to Plant City, where he continued his military service in the Plant City Army National Guard. It was a bit more common in those days to transfer from one branch of military to another in order to complete the required years of service. He and my grandmother, Elsie Greene, were high school sweethearts. They had remained in contact during his years at the Naval Academy and reconnected in earnest upon his return to Plant City, marrying in 1932. The union was certainly beneficial to Robert Wilbur, Sr. for a number of reasons.

Elsie Greene was, without question, a beautiful and intelligent woman. She came from a wealthy family, and her father was the general manager of Coronet, one of the largest employers of engineers in the area. My grandfather, of course, got a job with the company.

The Coronet Phosphate Company was in the business of mining phosphate from local lands, which was then processed, converted to animal feed, and sold to businesses and farmers. Construction on the processing plant and employee village began in 1906, and mining operations began in 1908. A major perk for the employees of Coronet was free housing. In the early 1900s it was not uncommon for large industrial companies to provide housing for employees. Personal vehicles were still relatively rare, and roadways were primitive. Having employees live where they worked was generally considered a win-win for both company and employee. The Coronet Village originally contained roughly seventy-five homes located on either side of one long street. It was a close-knit community with its own post office, grocery store, recreation facility, swimming pool, tennis courts, and nine-hole golf course, among other things. In addition to providing housing, the company paid all utilities and was responsible for the overall upkeep of the grounds.

The Wilburs, of course, lived at Coronet, and were an attractive and highly popular couple. Bob, a dashing Annapolis graduate and engineer, and Elsie, the beautiful and vivacious daughter of the plant manager. The young couple liked to party, and their social calendar was almost always full. They managed to find time, however, to begin construction of the perfect nuclear family, first welcoming my father in 1934, followed by my aunt Charlotte in 1938. With the ongoing expansion of the business, which required more employees and, therefore, more housing, Bob and Elsie moved from their pre-existing home to a newly constructed, larger house, just in time for the birth of their second child.

My dad's childhood was filled with all the normal everyday things that children of the South typically do. He and his best friends, Graham Austin and Jim-Tom Bauman (that's right. I said Jim-Tom, not just Jim *or* Tom, this was the South after all) went fishing, hunting, swimming, played football, golfed, played games, got into trouble together, and sometimes caddied at Coronet's golf course to make extra money. Graham was more the Monopoly player, hiker, hunter/fisherman, and Jim-Tom more the sportsman.

The unique and really special aspect of growing up in Coronet was its intimacy. All of my dad's friends lived there, so they were basically all on the same street, and were almost always together. According to relatives, my dad and his crew had a bit of a reputation in the Coronet community as mischief makers. One particular anecdote relayed to me by my dad went something like this: "There were about five or six of us who took the three mile walk to Plant City to go to the movies one afternoon. On our way back, we were nearly home when, I guess, boredom from the long walk set in. We started throwing rocks up on the roofs of tin-roofed houses along the way. Now, I don't think you've ever been in a house with a tin roof," he said to me, "but I can tell you that even a hard rain is noisy, so you can imagine what rocks might sound like. It wasn't too long before a police cruiser pulled up and asked us if we'd been walking along the road for a while. My friends all looked at me as if I'd make a reasonable spokesman and I blurted out, 'yeah, but we ain't been throw-in no rocks.' The cop just burst out laughing and told us to quit it and go home." When my grandparents caught wind of pranks like this, and others, my dad got a good old-fashioned southern ass-whipping. These instances were, of course, something of an embarrassment to a couple of such high esteem and good standing in the community.

The lineage of both the Wilburs and the Greenes is nearly purebred English, with just a bit of Dutch mixed in on the Wilbur side. Both sets of ancestors can be traced back as far as the seventeenth century in America. These are real blue-blooded WASPs. My grandparents, being the upstanding citizens they were, and having achieved a certain level of social status, felt it was incumbent upon them to teach their two children everything they thought fine upstanding people should know. Elsie was a virtuoso piano player, and Bob Sr., played the violin and sang a bit. Elsie often played for large audiences at the Coronet clubhouse where social gatherings were organized and impromptu karaoke nights were a fairly common occurrence. They taught both of their children to love and appreciate music. My dad learned to play the trumpet from a very young age, and continued to play throughout his teenage years, and even into college. He has an affinity and appreciation of all kinds of music, especially classical. Over the years I remember him and my mom occasionally attending the Metropolitan Opera in New York. In addition to fishing, hunting, and other manly things, his dad taught him about astronomy and horticulture. His paternal grandfather taught him to play gin, poker, and bridge, and to this day, even if nearly every other hobby or pursuit has fallen by the wayside, he still loves to play cards.

The person who, by far, made the biggest impression on my dad growing up, and of whom he has the fondest memories, was not a friend or relative. It was a man named Leonard P. Kory, who worked and lived at Coronet Village, and was the father of another one of dad's friends. Mr. Kory was a transplanted northerner who was employed by Coronet as a master mechanic, and my dad described him as a man who could make or fix just about anything. Mr. Kory was an aviation buff, and he loved to make and fly model airplanes. He was a patient and kind man who spent time nurturing a young boy's budding love of aviation, a love that would one day become a lifelong career. My dad remembers spending long hours with Mr. Kory on the grounds of Coronet making and flying the model planes. The two attended A.M.A (American Model Association) competitions together and took home a prize or two along the way.

The impact which Mr. Kory had on my father's life cannot be overstated. Upon his death many years later, Mr. Kory's widow, Margie, gave my dad one of her husband's favorite quilts. Living in our family, one would have to be extraordinarily obtuse to miss the symbolism in this one small gesture. Leonard Kory had offered my dad something in his youth that he was desperately seeking but was in terribly short supply: an adult mentor who generously gave of his time, not out of a sense of duty or obligation, like an item to be checked off a laundry list and quickly set aside, but simply for the pure enjoyment of fellowship. His interactions with Mr. Kory gave my father a kind of warmth and security every child needs. Mr. Kory has always been described through the years as a father figure to my dad, and his quilt remains in our family to this day.

Charlotte Wilbur was reared to be a true lady of the South. Anything and everything from the correct side of the plate to put the salad fork or the soup spoon, to the proper etiquette for hosting a dinner party, or afternoon social, or fundraiser, Charlotte learned it. Her mother sent her for piano lessons starting at age six and they continued through high school. She also learned to play the clarinet. The Wilbur children were given every advantage and were seemingly deprived of nothing, however, the consistent and overriding theme was that the children were expected to be independent and do their own thing. Family outings in the Wilbur household were not a regular occurrence, however, young Bobby and Charlotte both remember spending the last few weeks of most summers on the west coast of Florida in a rented cottage on the beach. My grandfather loved to fish; my dad, not so much. The kids swam and played on the beach by day and were expected to amuse themselves at night. Elsie and Bob, Sr., often partied with neighbors into the wee hours of the morning. It was okay for the kids to be seen but not heard.

In 1940, before America's entry into World War II, my grandfather was summoned to active duty. He was quickly deployed overseas at various locations before touching down in the Middle East. His permanent station was Persia (now Iran), where he worked with other army engineers on the railroad system among other things. He was highly intelligent, a committed and hard-working soldier, and an excellent engineer. My grandfather's wartime experience wasn't exactly miserable. In fact, he actually enjoyed his time overseas and would eventually achieve the rank of full bird colonel. When the war ended in 1945 he was, of course, given the option of returning state side. Now one would naturally expect that after five years away my grandfather must have rushed home to be with a family he'd been separated from and missed dearly. Well.... not exactly. He really liked Persia and the lifestyle it offered. He worked on interesting and challenging engineering projects during the day and partied with sheiks in their palaces at night. He decided to stay awhile. That is, until receiving a letter from his father-in-law, H.F. Greene, basically summoning him home. The crux of the letter was that if he failed to return home immediately, his job at Coronet would no longer be waiting for him. Robert M. Wilbur, Sr. did come back home. He resumed his life in Coronet Village, and returned to work at the Coronet Phosphate Company, where he would eventually become General Manager in 1955.

Elsie Wilbur was a stay at home mom. She kept herself busy with church activities, playing her piano, and chairing local fund raisers. Young Bobby and Charlotte were left in the care of a nanny named Evelyn, who cooked and cleaned the house, nursed them when they were sick, and, for all intents and purposes, was their primary caregiver. Beginning at age eleven, which would have roughly coincided with his father's return from overseas, my dad was sent away to summer camp in Wiley, Georgia. Until the start of high school he would spend his summers, save for the last few weeks, away from his home and family. The idea of spending months so far away from home at such a young age would have scared the hell out of me, but my dad never begged or pleaded with his parents to let him stay. He was told to go, so he went, and made the best of it. Below is a letter he wrote to my grandmother dated August 15, 1945:

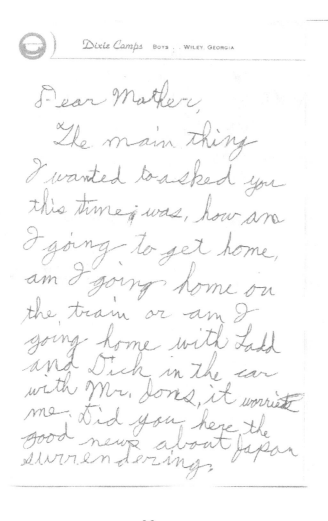

> This morning I ate three eggs. On every letter day we get candy.
>
> Love
> from
> Robert

Charlotte was likewise sent away to summer camp. At the age of thirteen she attended Skyland Camp for Girls in the mountains of Clyde, North Carolina. Unlike my dad, who at the ripe old age of eleven had no idea if he was taking the train home or hitching a ride in Mr. Jon's car with Ladd and Dick, Charlotte knew she was taking the train. Below is a letter she wrote to my grandmother on August 6, 1951. The notepaper she used you might expect from a young girl writing a letter to her mother. The content of the letter is another story, and it speaks volumes about the distant relationship between parent and child in the Wilbur household.

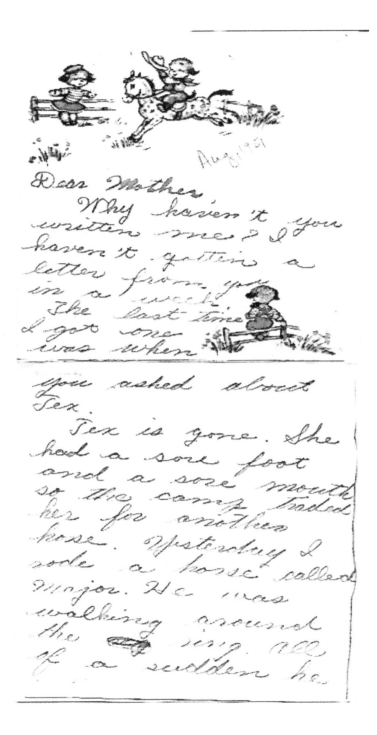

Aug 1951

Dear Mother,
Why haven't you written me? I haven't gotten a letter from you in a week. The last time I got one was when you asked about Tex.

Tex is gone. She had a sore foot and a sore mouth so the camp traded her for another horse. Yesterday I rode a horse called Major. He was walking around the ring. All of a sudden he started running and I wasn't prepared. I fell right off. I sat down. I was stunned for a minute but after that I got up and got back on. The riding counselor asked me if I was hurt but I didn't even feel it. They say that after you fall off a horse three times you are a good rider. I've got two more times to go.

Last night our cabin had a water fight and we also raided the icebox. We had lots of fun. Yesterday we sneaked to Clyde. Please wright.
Love,

Letter — Charlotte Gibson Card

Aunt Charlotte went to Plant City High School in Plant City, Florida, and was valedictorian of her class. She attended Duke University in North Carolina as a nursing major, and met her future husband, my uncle Gene, in July of 1959. She was between her junior and senior year at Duke, and the two were set up on a blind date. Like my grandfather, Gene Williams was an Annapolis graduate and engineer, who, like my grandfather, eschewed the Navy for another branch of military following his 1956 graduation. Gene wanted to be a flyer and thought the air force presented the best opportunity. However, soon after accepting his commission, he was told that his lack of 20/20 vision would likely preclude him from ever receiving his wings. He was convinced to become a navigator on the promise he might one day obtain a waiver for his imperfect sight and realize his dream of flying. Gene was based in North Carolina and worked on the B52 Bomber for a while, but was grounded when his hearing began to deteriorate. It was in North Carolina where he met and married my aunt, and where they started their very large family with the birth of my cousin Patsy in 1961. With the potential of a flying career now inextricably off the table, Gene wanted to go back to school. He was transferred to Wright-Patterson Air Force Base located just east of Dayton, Ohio, and attended Ohio State University, where he earned a master's degree in electrical engineering.

A three-year stint in Ohio was followed by a brief nine months in Colorado, followed by three years in Germany, then three years in Lubbock, Texas, where Gene earned his Ph.D. in electrical engineering. There was one last interim move to Albuquerque, New Mexico, before the family was finally able to settle down in Ocean Springs, Mississippi. At each stop the family grew. Child number two, Linda, was born in Ohio, David, in Germany, John and Jim in Texas. The very last of the twelve Williams children, Ricky, was born in 1982. All told my uncle Gene put in twenty-four years in the air force, followed by another twenty-eight in the private sector with

Ingalls Ship Building in Pascagoula, Mississippi. I suppose the prospect of a run of the mill thirty-year career was never a consideration for a man with twelve kids. He and my aunt worked hard all their lives, always for family, but I know neither one would have changed a thing.

Although Charlotte Williams never had the opportunity to put her nursing degree to use, it certainly came in handy over the years as she cared for the thirteen other members of her family. Unlike her own mother, whom, at a minimum, would have to be characterized as distant, Charlotte has always been a kind, caring, and patient mom, who lives for her children. It nearly broke her heart when her second youngest, Joey, was hit by a car and killed at the age of six while riding his bike in front of their house in Ocean Springs. All of my cousins, with the exception of Becky, who lives in Las Vegas, stayed pretty close to home. They're a close-knit group who have always counted on their mom for love, advice, for a sympathetic ear, and, later, for help with raising their own kids. Charlotte and Gene Williams have twenty-four grandchildren…and counting!

When my father's high school years rolled around, he was sent to Riverside Military Academy in Gainesville, Georgia. At this point, he was allowed to return home during summers to work in the drafting department at Coronet. The work required a lot of patience and, above all, strict attention to detail and was beneficial to him on several fronts. It helped to shape his strong work ethic, taught him responsibility, and further honed his already meticulous nature. He was proud of the work he did and having some extra walking-around money certainly didn't hurt. Those summers working at Coronet also made my dad realize something very important. He realized that he didn't want to work at Coronet.

My father never gave us a great deal of detail about his experience at Riverside. He studied military history, learned about important battles and about military strategy, and became familiar with various weapons during the course of his four years. There was the daily routine of reveille and drills and, of course, incessant inspections. Students were judged and rated on everything from how straight their shirts were tucked in, to the condition of their living quarters and personal possessions. I recall one specific anecdote he shared with me when I was a small boy. I had made my bed in the half-assed sloppy way that most little boys make their beds. After demonstrating the way he was taught to make a bed, my dad told me about how he was required to keep his room and make his bed while at Riverside. He said that his room was routinely inspected, and that his shoes had to be carefully placed in his closet, uniforms neatly hung, and all books, school supplies, and personal items had to be in their proper place. He said that his bed had to be made in such a way that the sheet and blanket were tucked so tight, "You could bounce a quarter off the bed." Thank God my sister and I were never held to such a standard. Military high school in the South in the 1940s doesn't exactly sound like a laugh a minute. It certainly wouldn't be the kind of high school experience any kid would wish for, but much like his banishment to summer camp year after year, my dad has never described the experience in a negative way. He simply accepted the situation for what it was and learned what he could from it.

The isolation from his family over the years, in both a geographical and emotional sense, no doubt played a part in shaping my father into the man he would become. At a very young age he was accustomed to being alone, and I'm sure it toughened him up, and probably, if he didn't already know it, made him understand the importance of self-reliance. His attendance at Riverside Military Academy certainly provided benefits. He gained a real appreciation and respect for the military, and when the time eventually came for him to actively pursue a flying career, his experience at Riverside would serve him well.

Following his high school graduation, my dad attended the University of Florida in Gainesville. At the insistence of my grandfather, who had contacted someone he knew in administration, he was housed in Thomas Hall, in a four-man suite, with three seniors. The idea being that he might get into less trouble living with older, more mature students. As it turned out, the logic employed by my grandfather backfired big time. The older boys were still young college kids who happily showed my father the ropes, and he took full advantage of every freedom that college offered. It was a feeling which, up to that point in his life, he had never experienced or imagined. The booze and the women flowed like a stuck open beer tap, and the bar never closed. He fooled around and partied like crazy, played trumpet in the school band, and, like just about every other college kid, had the time of his life.

When it came time to clear his head and focus on the future, he harkened back to his days with Mr. Kory, and the pure enjoyment he experienced building and flying model airplanes. Why not do it for real? In early 1955 he applied for Air Force Aviation Cadet training at Moody Air Force Base in Valdosta, Georgia. He was accepted into the program and began his training at Lackland AFB in San Antonio, Texas. A great deal of physical training accompanied six weeks of intense ground school, followed by primary flight training in Bainbridge, Georgia. My dad received his commission as a second lieutenant and was stationed at the old Sewart Air Force Base in Smyrna, Tennessee, where he flew a twin-engine C-119. His duties consisted mainly of troop transports and paratrooper drops between Sewart, Fort Bragg in North Carolina, Fort Campbell in Kentucky, and Fort Polk in Louisiana.

The life of a young air force pilot was hardly all work and no play. My father and his fellow airmen were young guys full of pent up energy and testosterone, and they were armed with weekly military paychecks that were burning holes in their pockets. These were the kind of guys who were fond of leaping without looking and they occasionally found themselves in some precarious situations. One such night happened in the spring of 1956. My dad and a friend, a fellow second lieutenant by the name of Graham, who also flew the C-119, decided to take a ride to Nashville, Tennessee. They'd heard about a really good bar, which among other things, had a reputation as a target rich environment for women. The problem was that a few hours before they planned to leave for the night and make the twenty-five-mile drive to Nashville, the two had already begun the process of way over indulging at the officer's club at Sewart with a group of like-minded young pilots. It had been raining on this particular night, and my dad was behind the wheel of his trusty two-door 1951 Chevy Power Glide. About halfway into the drive he lost control of the car which went into a sideways skid. The car was carrying enough speed that when its tires engaged a slightly dryer patch of pavement, it rolled over, twice. The car came to rest perfectly on all four wheels as if it was somehow maneuvered by a skilled pilot executing a double barrel roll.

Incredibly, neither man was seriously injured, and the incident escaped the attention of both military and local law enforcement. Needless to say, my dad and his friend never made it to Nashville that night. The accident scared the living hell out of Second Lieutenant Robert Wilbur, Jr., and its circumstances taught him a valuable lesson which would stay with him for life. Sure, he would continue to pursue a good time, and that pursuit would sometimes lead to over-indulgence. After all, he was a young military pilot, living, working, and traveling with other young military pilots. He was free and unattached and would travel the world and be exposed to exotic new places. He would, however, never again mix excessive alcohol consumption with driving.

After about a year at Sewart AFB, my father was transferred overseas. He spent his last three years in the military stationed at Evreux-Fauville Air Force Base in the small town of Evreux, Eure, France, just outside of Normandy, and about sixty miles west-northwest of Paris. It was an American base from 1954 to 1964, and home to the 317th Troop Carrier Wing. My dad flew the C-119 until the end of 1957, when the 317th began changing over to the new, and larger, C-130A Hercules. He loved flying both planes but gives a slight nod to the C-130A.

C-119 Flying Boxcar

About six months after his transfer to Europe, my dad was promoted to first lieutenant. He was flying in both the left and right seats depending on seniority and flight time. Most of the flying at Evreux involved trips down to Chateauroux, France, where freight or cargo would be loaded up and delivered to any one of a multitude of places around Europe, Africa, and the Middle East. One particular mission which stands out was the time he flew into Chateauroux, which was affectionately dubbed "Chad," and picked up cargo that he and his co-pilot were not allowed to see. It was loaded into the plane's cargo hold by a group of men under the watchful eye of military police. The pilots were ordered not to go into the cargo hold, and they never signed for whatever cargo they were carrying. After the five- or six-hour flight to Al Rasheed Air Base, located approximately eleven kilometers southeast of downtown Baghdad, Iraq, their C-119 landed and was quickly surrounded by a mob of cheering Iraqi soldiers. It turned out that the plane was carrying weapons and ammunition for the Iraqi Army. This was all part of America's strategy at the time to aid Middle Eastern countries in their efforts to stave off Soviet aggression. The Iraqi soldiers enthusiastically hugged both pilots after they deplaned and offered them beer and cigars, which they politely declined. My dad and his co-pilot only had a two-hour layover, otherwise, I'm sure they would have been all in.

Its close proximity to both Paris and the beautiful town of Rouen, located about forty-five miles to the north on the Seine River, made Evreux-Fauville an idyllic spot for a fun-loving young American military pilot. Road trips were made at every opportunity, and when harkening back to his days overseas, my dad gets lost in the reverie. The scenery, the beauty of the different cultures, and the great times he had with all his buddies, made the experience unforgettable. He looks back on his military career with a great deal of fondness, and why not? It was here that he learned the skills to do what he was born to do. He was born to fly. He traveled to exotic, romantic, and adventurous places all over Europe, North Africa, and the Middle East. He reveled in the camaraderie of his fellow airmen. They flew together, drank together, played cards together, and chased women together. Despite being an officer, he especially enjoyed hanging out with the enlisted men, and did so quite often. Their affinity for a raucous good time appealed to his simple, fun-loving nature, and his humble down-to-earth personality made him a favorite among the enlisted ranks. In addition, my father was, by his own admission, a fairly lousy poker player, and the enlisted men loved to take advantage of that fact, especially around pay day. I've often asked him why he didn't re-up when his term of service came to an end, and his response is simply that he felt it was time to settle down.

C-130 Hercules

Upon completion of his four years of military service, my father returned home, and his first order of business was finding a job. Eastern Airlines was a reputable carrier and based in Miami, Florida, so it made sense to give them a try. His first interview was in early August in Tampa, Florida. After his second interview in Miami, he was hired by Eastern Airlines as a co-pilot on August 17, 1959, after which he began six weeks of ground school and flight training.

Eastern conducted training for all its new employees in Miami, Florida, but new hires were almost always sent elsewhere, usually to the Northeast. As it turned out, following the completion of his flight training on October 6, 1959, my dad was told to head to New York. Although he was allowed a couple of days grace period before having to report for work, he decided to bypass a trip back to Plant City, and instead left immediately. There were logistics to think about, like finding a place to live in a new and unfamiliar place.

My dad crammed into a two-bedroom apartment in Flushing, Queens, with three other freshly minted Eastern pilots he had befriended during flight training. Bill Bussey from Atlanta, Bob McMurray from Baltimore, Maurice Mercer from Miami, and Bob Wilbur from the little town of Plant City, Florida, would all become the closest of friends. They were all fish out of water in the big city, away from the comfort and familiarity of friends and family, and with a new and challenging career ahead. The four of them got along like they'd known each other their whole lives. The tight living conditions were tolerable not only because the guys genuinely liked each other, but because they flew different schedules, and all four were rarely off at the same time. The hot-shot new pilots were all young and unmarried, and they lived the New York bachelor life-style to the hilt. They enjoyed bar hopping and carrying on together, while at the same time trying to stay out of each other's way when it came to matters of the female persuasion. Given that they were all co-pilots, they never actually flew together, but had that shared experience and the camaraderie associated with it. It had a very similar feel to his military service and was a great comfort to my father. Bill Bussey and Bob McMurray have since passed away. My dad's roommate, and best friend, in that long-ago shared apartment in Queens, was Maurice Mercer. I can remember vacationing with him and his family at Belle-Air Beach and in Key Largo, Florida, on numerous occasions in the 1970s and 1980s. He's alive and well, and he and my dad still correspond to this day. Interestingly, the two were born on the same day.

My dad started out on the small, forty passenger, twin engine, Martin-404, flying mostly upstate New York routes. On February 12, 1960, less than six months into their commercial aviation careers, Eastern Airlines furloughed my dad and his three roommates. In fact, their entire class was furloughed, given their lack of seniority. Such was the nature of the airline industry at that time. A little more than a month shy of his twenty-sixth birthday, my father found himself in a bit of a tight spot. Going home to Florida, after just six months of work, to sit out an indefinite lay-off would have been viewed as a failure in the eyes of my grandparents and would have been humiliating to my father. He had to find a way to stick it out. He interviewed with Northwest Airlines and was hired almost immediately. Northwest flew him out to their ground school in Minnesota, however, just after the completion of final exams for the DC-7, my dad was, once again, furloughed.

He returned to his apartment in New York and was able to find work as a ticket agent for Eastern Airlines at LaGuardia and Idlewild Airports. The pay was minimal, and in an effort to make ends meet, he worked a second job at an Air Canada ticket office in Manhattan. His three roommates found their own ways to survive the eighteen-month lay-off, and all were more than a little relieved when they were called back to work on August 17, 1961, exactly two years from the date they were originally hired.

My dad continued to fly co-pilot on the Martin-404, and became dual qualified on a number of larger, three-man crew aircraft over the next several years. As a dual qualified pilot, my dad was able to fly co-pilot as well as flight engineer. In a three-man crew aircraft, the cockpit included the two pilots (captain and first officer) and a flight engineer. The duties of the flight engineer included the interior and exterior pre-flight inspection, as well as checking all maintenance logs of the aircraft. During flight, it was the flight engineer's job to monitor all aircraft systems, diagnose problems, and, where possible, rectify or eliminate same. With the development of small and powerful integrated circuits and advances in computer and digital technology, the flight engineer became fairly obsolete in modern day aircraft. Planes now internally monitor and diagnose potential problems and inform the pilots via lights and buzzers on complex control panels. Starting in the mid-1980 most major airlines had begun to phase out aircraft utilizing a flight engineer. Below are photographs of a three-man cockpit crew, as well as most of the planes my father flew during his career with Eastern Airlines. With the exception of the DC-9, all of the planes were three-man crews.

3 Man Constellation Crew

Lockheed L-188 Electra

Martin 404

Lockheed L-1049 Super Constellation

Boeing 727

DC-8

Airbus A300

Lockheed L-1011

Douglas DC-9

***

Anita Marie DeCicco was born and raised in the coal mining town of Scranton, Pennsylvania. The area was, and for the most part still is, comprised of lower-middle-income Italian immigrants, and my mother's family was quite typical. She was the second of three daughters, born to Vincent and Mary DeCicco in 1940. The stories she told of her upbringing you've probably heard a thousand times from your own parents and relatives, especially after you complained about whatever hard time you might be having. The three sisters shared one bicycle, wore each other's hand-me-downs, and walked five miles to school in the rain and snow. There were countless stories and anecdotes of hard work, good times, lots of love, and the golden age of being a teenager in the 1950s.

Her family was without any real disposable income, and there was certainly no money for extras like travel. I can remember my mom recounting in great detail, and reverence, the very first time she saw the ocean when she was eighteen years old. She and a few girlfriends took a bus trip to Wildwood, New Jersey, and had the time of their young lives. People from Scranton, especially in my mother's era, tended to remain in the Scranton area to find jobs and to raise families of their own. The girls typically married and had children at a very young age. In 1963, at the age of twenty-three, my mom found herself single, unattached, and with two married sisters who were already beginning to expand their families. She had a full-time job she really liked, attended lots of weddings, including those of her two sisters, helped to care for her first nephew, Vinny, and for the children of her closest friends, and often had to answer the inevitable question, "When?" When would she finally meet a nice local boy, get married, and start a family of her own? You would imagine that being in this situation might have made her envious of those around her. On some level that might be true, but despite having a terrific job, and a family that she loved, my mom felt somewhat out of place in Scranton, and was more than a bit restless. She thought she might want to explore what life had to offer outside the confines of Scranton, Pennsylvania, and as luck would have it, an opportunity soon presented itself.

One day, while dropping off a friend at Wilkes Barre/Scranton International Airport, my mom saw a flyer advertising for Eastern Airlines flight attendants. An Eastern representative would be coming to an area travel agency in a month or so to conduct interviews. Not really imagining that anything would come of it, my mom went to the travel agency and met with the Eastern rep. She passed a written test and impressed her interviewer enough to be offered a three-day trip to Miami, Florida, where final interviews would be conducted. Having never traveled farther than Wildwood, New Jersey, and obviously never having flown, the prospect of a free trip to Florida, especially for someone like my mother, was a temptation she couldn't resist.

A week or so later, in the Eastern Airlines Training Center in Miami, Florida, twenty-three-year old Anita DeCicco had her second interview with a six-person panel. Truth be told, it was a bit more of a fashion show than an interview. She donned the skirt, heels, and pillbox hat, which comprised the flight attendant uniform, and paraded in front of the panel answering questions. As uncomfortable as it might be for a son to say, my mom, objectively, was a young, attractive, intelligent woman, who certainly presented well. That coupled with her first interview and initial test score and, low and behold, she was hired. A more accurate way to describe her status at that point would be to say that she was invited to try out. Sort of like a baseball player is invited to spring training. It was the very stringent six to seven weeks of training that would ultimately determine which girls would become Eastern Airlines flight attendants, and which would not.

They wanted her to start in two weeks, but my mom informed the powers that be that she needed more time. She was the office manager for James O'Brown, a big food broker in Scranton, who depended on her to handle the day-to-day operation of the business, and for whom she had a great affinity. Loyalty and responsibility to the man she worked for certainly played a role in her delayed start. That aside, my mom never really thought her trip to Florida would produce a job offer, and in addition to her feelings of excitement, she was both frightened and unsure about the prospect of leaving her job, her family and friends, and her hometown, for something so new and different. Even buying into the idea of a career as a flight attendant, the job itself was anything but guaranteed. Additionally, the pull of her Italian parents cannot be overstated, it was like gravity. However, her excitement at the prospect of starting a new adventure in a far-away place eventually won the day.

In February 1964, my mom found herself at the Miami Springs Villas in Miami, Florida, where Eastern Airlines housed their prospective flight attendants during the six-plus weeks of training. She was one of twenty-four candidates in her class. The girls, all of whom had to be unmarried, as per Eastern Airlines policy at the time, were provided room and board as well as transportation to the various training sites, but no salary. As per unwritten, but clearly understood airline policy of that era, all the women were young and attractive. My mom shared a villa with one roommate, and she describes the accommodations as "absolutely beautiful."

In addition to their basic duties as flight attendants, the women were trained in CPR, basic trauma, and a large array of emergency procedures. They had to become familiar with all the various planes in Eastern's fleet and were given proficiency tests on a daily basis. A minimum score of 90 was required on each and every test to achieve a passing grade. By the end of the six and a half weeks of training, twelve of the twenty-four girls had washed out. My mom finished second in the class with an overall grade of 96. It's no surprise that she requested to be based as close to home as possible, New York, New York.

In April 1964, after a brief stopover back home in Scranton, my mom moved to New York to begin her new career. She and classmate Joyce Snyder moved into the Briarwood Apartments on the Van Wyck Expressway in Queens. It was only a studio, and far too small, but it was still too expensive on their minimal salaries. Luckily, one of my mom's good friends from Scranton, a nice Italian girl named Ann Marie Noto, got a job as an x-ray technician at Lenox Hill Hospital in Manhattan. She squeezed into the already cramped apartment, and with the rent now being split three ways, the girls could afford to live, albeit with very little financial breathing room. My mom and Joyce were brand new hires and were so junior in the hierarchy of flight attendants that they were not able to bid trips. They flew in reserve status and were thus put on flights as the need arose and quite often on very short notice. The three young girls all worked long hard hours, but they enjoyed their new jobs and also found time to have some fun.

A couple of New York Yankee players, one much more famous than the other, also lived in the Briarwood Apartment Building. Roger Maris and relief pitcher Hal Reniff were roommates, and they befriended the girls. It was truly an exciting time, and over the years my mom has often recounted stories of hanging out with a number of famous Yankees, including Mickey Mantle and Whitey Ford. Ann Marie Noto dated and eventually married Hal Reniff, whose baseball career unfortunately ended in 1967 due to ongoing arm problems at the age of only twenty-nine. My mom recalls going out to dinner on occasion with Roger Maris, Hal Reniff, and Ann Marie, and she describes Roger as, "The nicest, most down to earth, and soft-spoken person you'd ever want to meet." Three roommates turned into four when Ann Marie Noto's sister, Elaine, joined the group, and the four girls moved into a small Manhattan apartment. When my mom met and began dating my father, she introduced him to some of the Yankee players, and he too had occasion to hang out and party with the famous athletes. There were lots of late nights, music and laughter, general carrying on, and good times had by all. My dad, being the way he is, wasn't terribly impressed by the fame and celebrity of his new found friends, especially since, like his son, he's a METS fan.

My father still has all his log books from the very start of his flying career. For that reason, all these years later, he can say with absolute certainty that he met my mother on September 6, 1964. Eastern Airlines Flight 307 was a Boeing 727, which departed JFK Airport in New York, bound for New Orleans, Louisiana. In addition to passengers, the flight carried six Eastern employees, three pilots and three flight attendants, including my mom, who were dead heading to New Orleans to do some charter work. At the conclusion of the flight, after all of the passengers had de-planed, my dad noticed an attractive young brunette struggling to remove her bag from an overhead compartment in the first class cabin. He watched her for a minute or so from his flight engineer seat before finally coming to the rescue.

They went through the normal dating ritual, hanging out with friends, going out to dinner, to concerts, and shows, and trips to Scranton to visit my mother's relatives. The two were married on April 28, 1965, at St. Lucy's Church in Scranton, Pennsylvania. All of mom's relatives and friends witnessed the nuptials. Her new in-laws, however, were not in attendance. Following their honeymoon in Bermuda, my parents went down to Florida where my mom met dad's family for the very first time. They threw a big reception for them at the banquet hall at Coronet. Given Eastern's policy that its flight attendants remain single, the marriage put an abrupt and premature end to my mother's budding career, but it didn't bother her in the least, as she certainly gained far more than she lost. She had found a good, honest, and hardworking man whom she loved, and with whom she would spend the rest of her life.

My parents moved into mom's old apartment building in Queens and wasted little time starting our family. My sister, Allison, was born in February 1966. With their New York apartment becoming a bit cramped, and with plans to expand their family, my parents began looking for a bigger place. Just over a year later, in March of 1967, our family made its move to the suburbs of northern New Jersey. They found a small, three-bedroom, one bath, Cape Cod, in a quiet residential neighborhood in Fair lawn. I came along in September of 1967.

By the fall of 1966, Dad was now a seven-year veteran pilot and able to bid trips more to his liking. In addition, rather than hopping from airplane to airplane, and from the co-pilot seat to the flight engineer seat, his equipment and position became somewhat more stable. From late 1966 until his promotion to captain in December 1969, he flew only two airplanes, the Boeing 727, and the Douglas DC-8-21, most often as co-pilot. The trips were typical Eastern fare, up and down the east coast and occasionally the Midwest.

In the airline industry a promotion to captain is an acknowledgment of competency and trust earned through years of experience. The captain is the pilot-in-command (PIC) and is responsible for all decisions regarding his aircraft. Not only does he make the, "Go, no go," call after reviewing weather reports and assessing the plane's airworthiness, he is the man responsible for all decisions made aboard the aircraft in flight. New captains are typically moved to smaller equipment, and my father was no exception. In December of 1969 he reported to the Eastern Airlines Training Center in Miami, Florida, to begin his training on the Douglas DC-9. This short to medium range twin engine jet was first produced in 1965, with the last rolling off the assembly line in 1982. Due to its great work ethic, versatility, and reliability, it spawned many variants over the years, including the popular MD-80, practically its clone, and still ever present in the airline industry today.

Fuel has always been a major expense for airlines so, in the interest of cost savings, nearly all of my dad's flight training took place in a simulator. After a few weeks of simulator work in order to familiarize himself with his new aircraft, and to re-acclimate to flying in the left seat again, my dad had his rating ride with the FAA Check-Airman. As you might have guessed he passed with flying colors. Now armed with four years of military training, and just over ten years of experience as a commercial pilot, my father was an Eastern Airlines Captain. His very first flight was a shuttle run from LaGuardia to Washington National Airport (Now Reagan National) on January 2, 1970.

Little did he know that in just two and a half short months all of his many years of training and experience, the repetition of flying thousands of hours, his cool unflappable demeanor, no doubt inherent in his DNA, but also developed over the course of his life, would be called upon in such a dramatic way, and would be absolutely vital to the survival of so many.

4. First Officer James E. Hartley, Jr.

Unlike my father, who was brought up in relative privilege, Jim Hartley came up hard. Born in Jacksonville, Florida, on November 15, 1939, he was given up for adoption at birth and was briefly a ward of the state until, at some point as an infant, he became the only child of his adoptive parents, James E. Hartley, Sr., and Sadie Hobbs Hartley of Miami, Florida. Jim grew up in a lower middle-class neighborhood on East 60th Street in Hialeah, just northwest of Miami, and has been described by friends and family as a wild kid with a big heart. He loved animals, the outdoors, and was a fiercely loyal friend. Jim Hartley, Sr. was a rather ill-tempered and overall unhappy man who was frustrated with the family's economic condition despite his hard work and sacrifice. In addition, he liked to drink, and had very little patience for his son's mischievous nature. He was the type of guy that my father probably would have described as "Spring loaded to the pissed off position." That state of mind, coupled with Jim Jr.'s propensity to find trouble, were something of a toxic mix. The father would often find an easy and accessible target for his frustration in the son. The abuse Jim suffered at the hands of his father certainly wasn't constant, but it reared its ugly head often enough, and was always present in the undercurrent of their relationship. Jim's mother, Sadie, was a pleasant woman, but she didn't possess a strong enough personality, by a long-shot, to offer a significant buffer between her husband and son.

James Sr. worked in a laundromat in Miami and was also a part-time mechanic. The hours were long and the pay was minimal. Sadie worked part-time to help make ends meet. I think it would be fair to say that neither parent was the type to overextend them self in an effort to corral or redirect their impish young adopted son. At some point during his primary school years, Jim was held back. He routinely ditched school during his middle and high school years to hang out with friends at the beach, or at the

36th Street pool, or at the local billiard hall. Jim was an active kid who loved to dive, spear fish, hang out at the beach, get into trouble, anything but go to school or sit around the house. Other than the occasional beating from his old man, there was no real guiding force in his life, nothing to motivate or to convince him to stay on the straight and narrow. He attended Edison High School in the rough and tumble Northwest Miami neighborhood known as, Little Haiti. Jim was a whopping five foot three and a hundred and five pounds soaking wet when he entered high school, and although he had a gentle disposition and was a friendly, fun loving kid, Jim didn't like to take any shit. Throughout his teenage years he had little choice but to learn how to handle himself, and he did just that. When he was backed into a corner Jim wasn't the type to run and hide, he came out swinging.

As his teenage years progressed, Jim spent less and less time in school and, according to family and friends, who were unable to elaborate further, he had some minor scrapes with the law. He was a pretty handy kid and a fast learner, who picked up some carpentry and plumbing skills, and eventually began working odd jobs to procure the funds necessary to keep his lifestyle afloat. Over and above hanging out at the beach, it cost money to shoot pool, drink beer, take out girls, and put gas in the car. Those were Jim's priorities, and more than sheer enjoyment, they provided for him a much-needed escape from the relative unhappiness of home and school. He pursued them with even more passion and enthusiasm than you might typically expect from a teenager. Jim was a high energy kid who loved having a good time, and like most teens, he gave little thought to the potential consequences of his actions.

On Christmas Day, 1956, a little over a month past his seventeenth birthday, Jim was arrested for reckless driving in Miami, Florida. He was sentenced to sixteen days in jail which he would serve in the Dade County Correctional Facility in Miami.

Other than the stated charge, no narrative or summary of the circumstances of the arrest exists, and nobody, friend nor family member, recalls the specifics of the incident. Anyone familiar with law enforcement will tell you that an incident resulting in the incarceration of a juvenile has to be pretty serious. Unless that incident is just one of a long list of transgressions that was the proverbial straw that broke the camel's back. Either way we can only speculate on the details. What is certain, however, is that Jim Hartley, Jr. was in some pretty deep shit. Although the beating he received from his father following the incident was most likely turned up a notch or two, it was basically nothing he hadn't endured before. The difference was the message sent, the way he felt in the aftermath of the physical and verbal altercations, after things cooled down, whether those feelings were real or perceived. Jim now felt that he was no longer welcome. No longer welcome to ditch school in pursuit of fun and freedom and a borderline juvenile delinquent existence. It was a path which would likely result in his dropping out of high school, leaving him with few future prospects. More important, he knew that his life couldn't continue as it had before. At just seventeen years old, and in the middle of his junior year of high school, Jim was at a crossroads.

For Jim Hartley, Jr. Christmas 1956 wasn't the merriest of holidays. He was a young man whose wings had officially been clipped. Jim knew that there were tough choices he had to make, and he also knew that the options available to him were limited. He never did return to Edison High School for the second half of his junior year. Instead, he made an effort to drum up more work for his handyman business, but he possessed neither the skills nor the maturity to make a real go of it. In addition, Jim Hartley, Sr. was well past having any further patience for his son. If he was no longer a high school student, his father wanted him out on his own. Over the previous year or so Jim had a few friends who talked about the possibility of joining the army. Some had older brothers, friends of older brothers, or cousins, or acquaintances who were in the military and, although he hadn't seriously considered it an option for himself, given the current state of things, the idea quickly began to grow on him.

At some point in March 1957, Jim, along with one of his running buddies, walked into the U.S. Army Recruiting Main Station, Room 344, Main Post Office, 300 N.E. 1st Avenue in Miami, Florida. It was there that he first sat down with a recruiter, a career army man who touted the benefits of military service. Their initial conversation lasted just over thirty minutes, but in that short period of time the man had little difficulty providing Jim with the small nudge required for him to fully buy in. They talked about lots of things, but what most appealed to Jim was the promise of travel, life-long friendships, camaraderie, and the relative freedom available to a young soldier. The savvy recruiter also discussed the various duty stations in America and abroad. Of course, the location of his station assignments couldn't be guaranteed, but Jim was told that he had a better than average chance of being stationed in Hawaii following basic training, if he made the request, and if he got through the program in good stead. For a kid from South Florida who loved the beach, the outdoors, the warm weather, and beautiful girls (what 17 year old kid doesn't?), this solidified a decision that was already pretty easy to begin with.

There were two potential sticking points to Jim Hartley, Jr's recruitment into the military. The first, of course, was the fact that he was only seventeen years old and needed parental consent. The second was his recent arrest and subsequent term of incarceration in Miami. As it turned out, neither one posed much of a problem at all. Jim's Christmas night reckless driving arrest was investigated by army personnel and was deemed "Not so significant as to preclude him from military service." On April 4, 1957, he received a waiver for the arrest and was found to be, "Acceptable for enlistment in the United States Army." That same day Jim Hartley, Sr. and his son took the short drive to 300 N.E. 1st Avenue in Miami. Jim Sr. was all too happy to sign the necessary consent form which would allow his seventeen-year-old son to join the army. Mom, Sadie, offered very little push back. In her heart of hearts she likely knew that it was her son's best option.

```
                    U. S. ARMY RECRUITING MAIN STATION
                         Room 344, Main Post Office
                    300 N.E. 1st Avenue, P.O. Box 1030
                              Miami, Florida

         341-Hartley, James Edward, Jr.                    4 April 1957

         SUBJECT:  Waiver of Juvenile Case


         TO:       Commanding Officer
                   United States Army
                   Recruiting Main Station
                   300 N.E. 1st Avenue, P.O. Box 1030
                   Miami, Florida



              1. The Juvenile Case against Mr. James Edward Hartley, Jr.
         has been investigated by the undersigned in accordance with paragraph 9e
         (b) AR 615-120, and has been found acceptable for enlistment in the United
         States Army.

              2. Documentary evidence on which this decision was reached is attached
         as inclosures hereto.

                   FOR THE COMMANDING OFFICER:


                                                  GEORGE T. WILLIAMSON, JR.
                                                  Master Sergeant, U. S. Army
                                                  Sales Supervisor

                   Approved


                                                  ELLIS A. STRICKLIN
                                                  Captain, Infantry
                                                  Commanding
```

James Edward Hartley, Jr. returned to fill out his DD-4 on April 8, 1957 (Service#ER-14-638-250). On the form he reported his occupation as, "Carpenter," with an average weekly salary of $63. Even allowing for the fact that his self-reported carpenter's salary was almost certainly exaggerated, as an enlisted man in the army at the lowly rank of PvtE-1 (Private), he was about to take a pretty significant pay cut. The pay scale at his level was around $81/month, in addition to a small monthly allowance of just over $50. He signed on for a minimum term of three years active military service. He would then be required to serve an additional two years in the ready reserves, followed by one year of standby reserve duty. After successful completion of his basic training at Fort Benning, Georgia, Jim was briefly stationed at Fort Lee in Virginia. Very soon after that, he was happy to hear that his request for station assignment had been granted. For weeks he had suspected, and was waiting and hoping, that he'd soon be on an army transport bound for Hawaii. He had heard that Fort Shafter was still under staffed, and a couple of his buddies had already been assigned there, but when his orders finally came through on August 31, 1957, Jim was both relieved and excited. He arrived at Fort Shafter in Honolulu, Hawaii, on September 17, and was assigned to the 10th Engineer Combat Battalion.

Army life was all about routine, especially during peace time. Jim was never deployed overseas, and, like my father, was lucky enough never to have seen combat. Among other duties assigned to him, Jim was a supply handler and a laundryman. He found combat training to be a welcome diversion, and he was good at it, eventually becoming an expert marksman. Even in 1957 the United States Army was forward thinking enough to allow its non–high school graduate enlistees to attend school while on active duty. Jim took full advantage of this and managed to earn his GED in 1958. Although it would probably be an exaggeration to say that Jim loved his time in the army, it would be inaccurate to say that he disliked it. The army taught him a modicum of patience, responsibility, and discipline. He saw it for what it was; his best option to escape a life that was, at worst, spinning out of control, and, at best, simply going nowhere. Jim was lucky enough to remain at Fort Shafter throughout the remainder of his three years of active duty. By army standards the atmosphere was fairly laid back and the base was right smack dab in the middle of paradise.

Not surprisingly, off duty times were spent off base, and the surrounding area offered such a variety of things to do and see that a young soldier didn't exactly have to put together a search party to find a great time. The beaches, the fishing, the diving, and the overall beauty of Oahu were, of course, second to none, and they made a young Jim Hartley feel a bit closer to home. The nightlife in and around Honolulu was no slouch either. Not only did the locals love to party, but the area was home to loads of military personnel from Fort Shafter, Pearl Harbor, Hickam Air Force Base, and others, all within a fifteen- to twenty-mile radius.

It was here, at one of the area nightclubs he frequented, that Jim met his first wife, Shirley Abrahano, in the fall of 1958. She was one of the many locals on the Island of Oahu who was of Philippine decent, and she was born and raised in Hawaii. The night club where they met played honky-tonk music upstairs and jazz downstairs, and while Jim might have preferred the music on the second floor, he found the scenery more pleasing on the first. Jim and Shirley were young and, not only did they share a strong physical attraction, they also had many interests in common, and it was all too easy for them to fall in love in such an idyllic environment. They dated and eventually married in the summer of 1959 in the Chapel at Ft. Shafter. Shirley continued to live with her parents, while Jim, of course, remained at his barracks. The two spent a great deal of time together and had many long talks about where they would settle down after Jim's three-year term was up. Shirley's family and friends, her roots, were in Hawaii, and she was understandably apprehensive about leaving it all behind. Although Jim loved the beauty and serenity of his new wife's home state, he couldn't see himself settling down and raising a family there. He wanted to return to Florida, and, in the end, he convinced her to make the move.

Jim Hartley, Jr. completed his term of active military service in early April of 1960. On March 29, 1960, he boarded a C130 Hercules at Hickam Air Force Base and traveled to the U.S. Army Petroleum Center in Oakland, California. He spent about a week at USAPC-Oakland, during which time he was met by Shirley, who took a commercial flight from Oahu. A few days later they took a cross country train to Florida, and soon after, settled into a rented house at 428 NW 45th Street in Miami. Jim was assigned to the VI U.S. Army Corps (Reserves). His reserve unit was called up on a number of occasions over the following three years, but he was never deployed overseas. Other than call ups, and meeting his reserve duty and training obligations, Jim lived his life, once again, as a civilian.

He and Shirley welcomed their first child, Debra, on January 11, 1961. Jim stayed busy over the next several years searching for his place in the world. He moved in and out of a variety of different jobs, working as a maintenance man, carpenter, garbage truck driver, mechanic, anything to make ends meet. The pressure to secure a solid job with an ample and steady income was ramped up when Shirley gave birth to their son, James Allen Hartley, on February 16, 1963. Jim was honorably discharged from the army on April 30, 1963, as a SP4-E4 (Specialist). His veteran status would give him an edge when he applied to become a fireman in Hialeah in 1963.

For many reasons the job was a terrific match for Jim. It obviously appealed to his sense of adventure and he always felt good when he was helping other people. He loved the camaraderie he had with the other firemen, and his outgoing personality made him lots of friends. Jim was a real doer who could be fairly characterized as uncomfortable with idle time. His need for perpetual motion, and his drive to succeed, only needed to be pointed in the right direction. While these traits would ultimately bear fruit in the form of his dream job, for Jim, career success came at a price. He would often work shifts at the firehouse that kept him away from home for three or more consecutive days. In addition, he picked up whatever work he could on the side, even working as a part-time salesman for a local kitchenware company. Jim had an insatiable work ethic which, when coupled with the fact that his young man's desire to pursue a good time had barely waned since his teenage years, left precious little time for a home life. I suppose that, stereotypically, firemen like to party and chase women, and Jim was no exception. His marriage to Shirley slowly deteriorated over time and they eventually divorced in June of 1965.

One of Jim's running buddies was fellow firefighter Jerry Simpkin, who just happened to own a little Piper J-3 Cub. He took Jim up in the little two-seater one day and let him take the controls for a while. It was love at first flight. Jim started hanging around Jerry quite a bit, and they'd spend lots of time at Tamiami Airport in Miami, where he kept his plane. Jerry had learned to fly at Kendell Flight School at the airport, and he introduced Jim to everyone he knew, including several young flight instructors who were just about Jim's age. There was a positive, energized, atmosphere around the flight school at that time, and it was a place where Jim felt right at home. In the mid-1960s there was a serious pilot shortage in the airline industry. Airlines were expanding, purchasing new routes and new planes, and they needed qualified pilots to fly them. Experienced military pilots, such as my father, were too scarce in number, and airlines had little choice but to try to find qualified pilots in the private sector. They often looked for pilots at small private flight schools, such as Kendell, and would hire pilots with as little as two hundred hours of flight time, so long as they had a commercial rating. Jim Hartley was always fascinated with airplanes and flying, but, until meeting Jerry, and spending time with the guys at the airport, he never thought for a moment that becoming a professional pilot could be a possibility for him. In early 1964, still working as a full-time firefighter, among other things, Jim started taking flying lessons.

He became close friends with flight instructor Jim Hamilton. The two men carried the same initials, shared a love of flying, and were just about the same age, but they came from totally different backgrounds. Jim Hamilton hailed from Ohio and graduated from Muskingum College in New Concord in 1962 with dual degrees in math and chemistry. During his four years of college he took flying lessons and got his private license just before graduation. Heart set on becoming a commercial pilot, he applied to, and was accepted into the Ohio Air National Guard. Obviously not having the requisite ratings to be a pilot in the Guard, he flew as a navigator, and gained valuable experience. Jim continued taking flying lessons at a local flight school but soon after moved to the Miami area and transferred to the Florida Air National Guard. He got a full-time job at Miami-Jackson High School as a math teacher and religiously continued his pilot training on weekends. He got his instrument and commercial ratings, and by early 1964 became a certified flight instructor. Jim left his job teaching high school math for a full-time flight instructor position at Kendell. Flying was all Jim really wanted to do and he knew he needed to accrue as many flight hours as possible to become an attractive candidate to an airline.

Although their respective backgrounds could hardly have been more different, the two Jims couldn't have been more alike in their relentless pursuit of an aviation career. Jim Hartley showed an amazing aptitude for flying and he was hungry to learn and advance his ratings. In no time, despite his multitudinous work and family obligations, Jim earned his private pilot's license, and by mid-1965, right around the time his divorce was finalized, he added an instrument rating. Following his divorce from Shirley, he moved into a small apartment on S.W. 9th Street in Miami. The split wasn't by any means amicable, and visitation certainly wasn't made easy, but despite the challenges he faced, including his incredibly busy schedule, Jim made every effort to see Debra and James as often as he could. These were tumultuous times for Jim, but they were happy times nonetheless. He no longer felt like he was running in place, spinning his wheels in pursuit of a goal that didn't quite fit. Gone was any shadow of doubt as to what direction he should apply his seemingly bottomless level of energy. It provided a clarity of mind he was unaccustomed to, and for Jim, it was liberating.

On January 21, 1966, Jim earned his commercial pilot rating, and just six weeks later, on March 7, 1966, he earned his airman certificate as a flight instructor. Jim was able to catch on at Kendell Flight School as a full-time instructor, and he left his job at the Hialeah Fire Department.

TEMPORARY AIRMAN CERTIFICATE

Certificate No. 1666208CFI

This certifies that JAMES EDWARD HARTLEY, JR.
180 S. W. 9 STREET
MIAMI, FLORIDA

Date of Birth: 11/15/39 — Height: 69 in. — Weight: 155 — Hair: BROWN — Eyes: BLUE — Sex: M — Nationality: U.S.A.

has been found to be properly qualified and is hereby authorized in accordance with the conditions of issuance on the reverse of this certificate to exercise the privileges of

FLIGHT INSTRUCTOR (EXPIRES 3/31/68)

Ratings and Limitations: AIRPLANE
VALID ONLY WHEN ACCOMPANIED BY PILOT CERTIFICATE NUMBER 1666208

Date of Issuance: 3/7/66
By Direction of the Administrator: W. R. MONTGOMERY
Examiner's Designation No.: 80-05

Form FAA-1710 T (5-59)

TEMPORARY AIRMAN CERTIFICATE

Certificate No. 1666208CFI

This certifies that JAMES EDWARD HARTLEY, JR.
180 S. W. 9TH ST.
MIAMI, FLORIDA

Date of Birth: 11-15-39 — Height: 69 in. — Weight: 150 — Hair: BROWN — Eyes: BLUE — Sex: M — Nationality: USA

has been found to be properly qualified and is hereby authorized in accordance with the conditions of issuance on the reverse of this certificate to exercise the privileges of

FLIGHT INSTRUCTOR (EXPIRES 5-31-68)

Ratings and Limitations: AIRPLANES AND INSTRUMENT
VALID ONLY WHEN ACCOMPANIED BY PILOT CERTIFICATE NUMBER 1666208

Date of Superseded Airman Certificate: 3-7-66
Date of Issuance: 5-11-66
By Direction of the Administrator: J. L. SMITH

Form FAA-1710 T (5-59)

Soon after, in April of 1966, Jim Hamilton was hired by Eastern Airlines as a second officer on the Electra, based in Atlanta Georgia. The two friends would stay in close contact, Hamilton always offering sage advice and a positive sounding board for Hartley. He knew a professor at Dade County College and suggested that Jim enroll in a special high school program they sponsored. The thought being that with a high school diploma, rather than a GED, Jim might look more attractive to the airlines. He never did get his high school diploma, and nobody remembers whether he ever enrolled in the school. Jim did, however, have the good fortune of giving flying lessons to a young man named Don Landry, Jr., who absolutely loved him. The two hit it off like brothers and spent a good bit of the summer of 1966 flying airplanes together. Don Landry, Sr., was a former chief pilot and current executive with Eastern and being in the good graces of a man in his position was beneficial in speeding up a process that was already inevitable. Sooner rather than later, Jim would get to fly with the big boys.

On October 3, 1966, Jim Hartley, Jr. was hired by Eastern Airlines with little more than three hundred hours of total flight time in single engine propeller airplanes. He would have a much longer training row to hoe than did my father, who had flown multi-engine heavy equipment, was military trained, and had just shy of two-thousand hours of flight experience when he was hired by Eastern. Following an intensive six-month training program in Miami, Jim, like so many new hires, found himself based in New York. He began his flying career as a second officer on the DC-8. Dual qualified as a flight engineer and co-pilot, Jim "seat swapped" with other young pilots in the three-man cockpit of the DC-8 in order to get valuable flight time in the co-pilot chair. Initial training was all done in simulators, but actual hands-on flight training was done on real passenger flights via seat swapping under the watchful eye of the captain. Talk about on-the-job training!

Unlike my father who was single and had nothing keeping him from moving twelve hundred miles away, Jim Hartley had a family in Miami, and he wanted to see Debra and James as much as he could. He remained in Miami and commuted to the New York/New Jersey area, flying out of all three major airports. As high energy as Jim was, spending that amount of time on airplanes is a grind for anyone, and it wore on him. What's more, he wasn't finding adequate time to spend with his kids anyway, and whatever time he was able to carve out always seemed rushed. After about a year of this, Jim found a way to rectify the situation. A flight instructor position in the Miami training center became available, and it was open to qualified second officers even at Jim's lowly seniority level. He really enjoyed his time as a flight instructor at Kendell and this seemed like the perfect solution to his domestic dilemma. What's more, flight instructors kept their seniority number, and were required to fly the line every few months, which would keep Jim in the air. The job entailed training new hires as flight engineers on the DC-8, and Hartley was fortunate enough to be selected. Jim Hamilton once told me that he wasn't sure what Jim Hartley enjoyed more, flying or teaching, and with his new job he would get to do both.

Jim liked the work, and with regular hours he got to spend more time with Debra and little James. However, given his hyper-driven personality, settling down and not having to jump on and off airplanes and frenetically run from place to place, felt like an unnatural state to Jim. He went back to selling kitchenware door to door. It was while working this part-time job that he met and began dating Rebecca Pamplin. Jim's ex-wife, Shirley, had been dating a man named Peter, whom she would marry and quickly divorce. Jim and Becky got engaged at some point in 1968 and, not long after, Shirley took the kids back to Hawaii. Jim was torn up about the move. He requested a transfer back to full-time flying which meant that he would, once again, be based in the New York area. With nothing keeping him in South Florida, and with a willing fiancé, Jim and Becky moved north and settled into an apartment in Fort Lee, NJ. Jim would again fly as a second officer on the DC-8 and get time in the co-pilot chair whenever he could.

Jim and Becky got married in the summer of 1969, and in the fall he was promoted to 1st officer on the Boeing DC-9. Following six weeks of training back in Miami, he returned to Fort Lee and began flying the shuttle, mostly from Newark to Boston and Newark to Washington, D.C. Jim met my father when they were paired together on the Eastern shuttle flight from Newark to Boston on March 3, 1970. It would be safe to say that the two hit it off immediately. They'd fly together another five times, including March 17, 1970, and it was always the same double round trip from Newark to Logan International.

The night before the infamous flight, Jim Hamilton got a chance to talk to Jim Hartley, whom he hadn't seen or spoken to in quite a while. Hamilton was living in the Atlanta area and the two hadn't heard from each other in at least six months or so. Jim, to his regret, hadn't been able to attend Jim and Becky's wedding. Given their varying schedules, ever evolving lives, and lack of proximity, they just weren't able to connect. On March 16, 1970, Hamilton was on a layover in Newark and was hanging around flight-ops before departing for Atlanta, via Miami. Sometime between 6:30 and 7:00 p.m., Jim Hartley and my dad were between legs two and three of their Newark to Logan shuttle run. When they ran into each other in flight-ops both men were glad to see each other and got to spend about a half hour catching up.

Hartley and Hamilton had only known each other for six years, and Jim Hartley has been gone for forty-nine years and counting, yet Jim Hamilton still remembers and appreciates their friendship. He describes his friend as someone akin to a shooting star. He said that Jim burned so brightly and had such an amazing impact on those around him, but that his light was extinguished far too quickly.

5. John Joseph Divivo, Jr.

Most great stories have an element of good vs. evil, heroes and villains, tales of everyday men and women who are thrust into incredible situations and are forced to find a way to dig deeper and perform better than they ever thought possible in order to save the day. The villains faced by these extraordinary men and women are, all too often, sick in mind and heart, and their ultimate goal can be death on a catastrophic scale. The hijacking of Eastern Airlines Flight 1320 is just such a story.

Unfortunately, we hear about this type of evil on the evening news every other day it seems. There are random shootings at schools, movie theaters, and shopping malls. Airports, bus terminals, and crowded tourist attractions are blown up in an attempt to kill as many innocents as possible. Even police officers have been specifically targeted by shooters. These types of murderous acts are born out of mis-guided religious zealotry, or hatred, or insanity, plain and simple. The latter, I think, is what confuses and disturbs us most. It's not that any reasonable person can empathize with or understand how a person could commit mass murder in the name of religion, or out of pure hatred. However, we can at least take measure and understand that, however warped the motive might have been, it was still a motive. But the murderous acts committed by those who are mentally unhinged, when they are seemingly devoid of any motive whatsoever, always seem to shake us to our very core.

John Joseph Divivo, Jr., was born on June 24, 1942, in Englewood, New Jersey. He was one of five children born to Angelina and John Joseph Divivo, Sr. He and his two brothers, Frank and Joseph, and two sisters, Dianne and Rose, grew up in Cliffside Park and West New York, New Jersey. There doesn't appear to be anything terribly unusual about John's early childhood, although he was certainly less than a motivated student, dropping out of school after just the eighth grade. At the age of fifteen or sixteen he began working at Palisade Amusement Park, in Palisade Park. He worked various jobs at the amusement park and was generally considered hard working and conscientious. Former employer and restaurant owner, Fred Nasif, said, "In all the time he worked for me he was a quiet kid who did his job well and expected everyone around him to do their jobs well. The only time he ever got mad was if he thought somebody else was loafing and making more work for him. He was always fine until somebody got him mad." Nasif went on to note that his former employee had been particularly sensitive about his teeth. "They weren't particularly good to begin with, and he just about polished them off that time he put a bullet in his head. That's why he didn't smile very much."

Divivo was twenty-seven years old at the time of the hijacking and living in an apartment at 6009 Boulevard East in West New York with his mother and three siblings. He had now been working steadily for John McCoy at Palisades Bullpen, Inc., the company which ran the game concessions at Palisades Park, since approximately the age of twenty-one. FBI Investigators worked diligently and tried desperately to put together some kind of motive following the hijacking. Interviews of Divivo's co-workers (all names redacted in FBI reports) produced consistent information to say the least. They all described him as a quiet, nondescript, and pleasant enough guy whose nickname was, "The professor," due to the bushy beard he always wore. None of the subjects interviewed ever knew Divivo to have a significant other, or a particularly close friend, and none of them knew him to have any friends outside of work. No one ever described Divivo as a good friend, just a friend, but they all said he was a nice guy and, to a man and woman, were genuinely surprised when they learned what he'd done. Divivo's family members were unable to name any specific friends, and they never knew him to have a girlfriend.

His mom and siblings would only say that he hung around with his co-workers at the amusement park.

In the days leading up to the hijacking, Divivo spoke to several friends/co-workers who indicated that he told them he was going to California to live with a relative and look for work. He said he first planned on going to Boston to party for a few days and to collect money owed to him by a friend. He had apparently visited a friend in Boston in 1969 to whom he had lent a small sum of money. Angelina Divivo confirmed that her son had visited an unknown friend in Boston the prior year, but she could not provide any more detail.

Despite living in the same relatively small apartment with her son, Angelina Divivo told investigators that she hadn't seen him since February 15, more than a month before the incident. Members of his immediate family said they had no prior knowledge that he was planning to go to Boston, nor that he planned to move to California to live with a relative. Neither his mother, nor his two brothers, or sister, could recall having any relatives in California. Suffice it to say, it does not appear that, on the surface at least, the Divivo clan was a very tight knit group. Every member of his family, every friend, acquaintance and co-worker interviewed by the FBI denied knowing that Divivo was in possession of a firearm, or that he planned on hijacking Eastern Airlines Flight 1320. Why then? A look into Divivo's troubled history will no doubt shed some light on why he might try to harm himself. However, it certainly falls short of explaining why he would be so determined to take so many innocent lives with him.

On August 26, 1958, a sixteen-year-old John J. Divivo, Jr. was found lying in a pool of blood outside of 278 Knox Avenue, Palisade Park, New Jersey, a .38 caliber revolver next to him. Police rushed him to Englewood Hospital where doctors frantically treated his life-threatening injuries. A bullet entered above his right ear canal and lodged in the soft tissue of his left parotid area. In layman's terms, he had shot himself in the head. Removing the bullet would have caused further damage, if not death, so it was left right where Divivo intended it be, but without the desired result. After more than a month in the hospital, followed by nearly a full year of physical therapy, he would survive his attempted suicide.

Survive, yes, but he certainly didn't walk away unscathed. The self-inflicted gunshot wound caused permanent nerve damage and a partial paralysis of his left side. It affected his eyesight and caused him to walk with a limp. Obtaining records of juveniles who have spent time in psychiatric facilities is a difficult, if not impossible, task. During the course of their investigation, the FBI was rebuffed in their attempts to get records from Bergen Pines County Hospital in Paramus, New Jersey, regarding John J. Divivo, Jr. His suicide attempt at the age of sixteen was common knowledge among his friends at Palisade Amusement Park, and, of course, his family. It was apparently motivated by his extreme despondence over being rejected by a girl. His life would obviously never be the same. A serious car accident in 1967 led to further debilitating head injuries, as well as a broken arm. More heartbreak would follow.

According to newspaper reports, Divivo's sister, Rose, had suddenly, and tragically, passed away in 1968. The cause of death was not reported. Detailed FBI reports on the hijacking indicate that John Joseph Divivo, Sr. died of a heart attack in New Jersey State Prison on March 17, 1968, exactly two years before the hijacking of Eastern Airlines Flight 1320. The offense for which he was sent to prison does not appear in any data base, nor could the information be ascertained via an Open Public Records Act request submitted to the New Jersey State Police.

Divivo's suicide attempt at the age of sixteen crippled him physically. Living with what he had done to himself, feeling the constant reminders in the form of a severe limp, limited eyesight, a weak and scarred body, and the looks he must have gotten from those around him, could only have exacerbated an already frail mental makeup. Add to that the heartbreaking loss of his father, who was serving time in state prison, and the death of his kid sister, and is it really a stretch to consider that Divivo, Jr. might try to end his life for a second time?

The question that begs an answer is, why the drastic change in M.O.? Reports indicated that he had been alone when he shot himself in the head on August 26, 1958. Divivo was consistently described by family, friends, and acquaintances as a pretty nice guy. His former employer, Fred Nasif, indicated that he got, "mad," when co-workers loafed around, but stopped well short of characterizing him as violent. West New York Police indicated that Divivo was never a problem to them. His one and only encounter with police came in 1963, when, at the age of twenty-one, he purchased a trumpet which was stolen from a local high school. Why now would he seek out such a sensational death? And why now would he be willing to kill so many others in the process?

There is no information available on how sixteen-year-old John J. Divivo, Jr. got his hands on the .38 caliber revolver he used in his first attempted suicide. However, the nearly identical gun he would use less than twelve years later aboard Eastern Airlines Flight 1320 is another story. A trace of the serial number on the .38 caliber Colt Positive Revolver revealed that it was reported lost, or stolen, by its North Bergen, New Jersey, owner on July 30, 1969. In a statement made to investigators following the hijacking, the owner of the gun, who happened to be a North Bergen police officer, denied knowing John Joseph Divivo, Jr. and could not speculate as to how, or why, his gun was taken. In his statement following the incident, Divivo denied stealing the gun. He told investigators that in July or August of 1969, he met an unknown individual in West New York and bought the gun from him. He claimed that he had no particular reason for buying it. When questioned by investigators as to his motive for the hijacking, Divivo repeatedly said that he never intended to hurt anyone. He said he wanted to get attention so he could be put away because he was, "cracking up."

Knowing what you know up to this point, do you have even the slightest doubt as to the premeditated nature of the hijacking and the malice of forethought in the mind of John Joseph Divivo, Jr.? Further, is there any doubt that his own death, and therefore, the deaths of everyone on board the flight, was the desired outcome? If so, consider the following: Divivo bought two flight insurance policies through Mutual of Omaha, for which he paid premiums of 50 cents each. The policies were for $15,000 and $20,000 respectively, and the beneficiaries were two female friends from Cliffside Park, New Jersey (names redacted). A few days after the hijacking, each woman received a letter from Divivo, along with a copy of their respective insurance policy. Neither were paid off.

The contents of his luggage, as well as the items he brought on board the aircraft, are strange to say the least. He checked one tan vinyl suitcase containing:

- An 11-and-a-half by 19 inch wooden sign painted a grayish color with the following words painted in black: "Pro J.J. Divivo born June 24, 1942 died Oct 31, 2015 M dig it R.I.P?"

- A long computer type form containing sixteen pages, each measuring 8-and-a-half by 11-and-a-half inches. The pages were marked, "Astroflash" and contained astrologic data concerning himself and referencing his birthdate, June 24, 1942.

- A total of nine books including; *Alchemy Ancient and Modern* by Stanley Redgrove, *Satanism and Witchcraft* by Jules Dichilet, *Geography of Witchcraft* by Harry G. Wedeck, *The Encyclopedia of Witchcraft and Demonology* by Russell Hope Robbins, *The Tarot Revealed* by Eden Gray, *Witches and Sorcerers* by Arkon Daranl, *The Last Laugh* by John Trotta, *A Pictoral Anthology of Witchcraft, Magic and Alchemy* by Emile Grillot DeGivry, and *The History of Witchcraft* by Montague Summers.

It's quite obvious from his choice of reading material, in addition to some of the other items found, that John Divivo had more than a passing interest in astrology and the occult. There were some letters written to him by friends, postcards, an astrology chart, three paper plates, two napkins, and one matchbook. There was no clothing of any kind found in his suitcase. The suitcase also included a picture of his father, John Joseph Divivo, Sr., who died exactly two years earlier on March 17, 1968. Did he attempt to commit suicide and mass murder on this date as some kind of twisted homage to his late father? Why else would he have picked this particular date?

Several items were found on and around Divivo's seat, 22D. On the seat was a black Kodak camera case with an empty seven-inch gun holster concealed inside. A wooden walking cane was leaning against seat 22D and a box of tarot cards was under the seat. Other items were found within the pockets of his coat, which he had left on his seat prior to being escorted to the cockpit by Sandy Saltzer. In addition to innocuous items such as gum, keys, and loose change, there was a 6- by 4-inch green vinyl bag containing thirty-four rounds of .38 caliber ammunition. There was also a letter in an envelope addressed to, "Professor John," which read:

Hi Prof., as I was looking in the card store, I was thinking this saying is so true. Oh when you open this card it will be St. Patty's day. A little advise from a <u>dude</u> [the word dude underlined], to survive life you must be strong, you put down to much by your own self. If only you didn't think life's a hassle. Take it, its the way you want it. Prof., look at me, I have fun all the time. I bring people down before they get me down. So while your in the air think, remember, your loved by all of us.

Peace & Love
(name redacted)

Syntax errors aside, the letter appears to be from a friend trying to cheer up someone he or she thought was clearly depressed. In the same coat pocket there were five, "In Loving Memory Cards," four of the cards were marked, "John Divivo died March 17, 1968."

And so it was that on the afternoon of March 17, 1970, on the second anniversary of his father's death, John Joseph Divivo, Jr. visited his friends at Palisade Amusement Park to say goodbye. Then he made his way to Newark Airport to board a plane.

6. The Flight Attendants

Christine Dorothy Peterson:

Christine Peterson was born in Buffalo, New York, on August 10, 1945. Her father, Henry, was a career army man and proud World War II Veteran. He worked at the Connecticut Street Armory as a maintenance manager for the 174th Regimental Armory in Buffalo, following his overseas deployment. Her mom, Isabella, was born in 1909 and struggled through the Great Depression as a young woman. She and Henry met, married, and started a family rather late in life for the times, and were both thankful for whatever grace God gave them. Isabella gave birth to their first child, Vernon, in 1939, and two more children would follow over the next six years. She was a superfluous and frugal stay-at-home mom. Cooking, cleaning, making and mending clothes, nursing her children and husband in sickness, she was a kind and sympathetic ear, and the overall glue of the family.

Christine's early years were spent in the Sheridan Housing Projects in Tonawanda, New York, outside of Buffalo. It was a hard scrabble life, and one which taught young Christine and her two older brothers, Vernon and Louis, the value of hard work and perseverance. With these characteristics on full display, the family worked their way out of the projects and into a home of their own in Buffalo. The house at 200 Loring Avenue was purchased by Henry and Isabella from the Catholic Church.

Christine was a quiet, slightly pudgy child, and was the youngest in the neighborhood. She's described by friends and family as having a quality about her, an inner toughness, that allowed her to keep up with the older kids. Her best friend, Marjorie Murphy, lived next door, and the two spent what seemed to be every waking hour together. Christine was two years younger than Marjorie and followed her everywhere. As children they played with dolls, rode bikes, played badminton, hop scotch, tag, and all the other things average kids do. They both graduated from Bennett High School and attended Bryant & Stratton Business Institute in Buffalo. According to Marjorie, "So many of the girls in our area went to Bryant & Stratton to learn secretarial, book keeping, and basic accounting skills. It was the best way to get an office job."

After completing school, Christine found a job in the offices of a local department store, Adam Meldrum and Anderson, and remained at home with her parents. Older brothers Vernon and Louis, both military men, had moved away and were busy pursuing careers and personal lives of their own. At the age of twenty Christine found herself living at home with her mom and dad, having a job she didn't particularly like, a boyfriend she liked only a bit more, and was staring at a future she saw as filled with limitations. Neither friends nor family can recall how the idea of a career as a flight attendant got into her head, but once it did, there was no turning back. Christine worked and studied hard to make it through the competitive flight attendant training program at Eastern Airlines. She earned her wings in mid-1966, just a few months shy of her twenty-first birthday.

Christine thrived in her new job. She found that she absolutely loved to travel, and the feeling of freedom which came with the job allowed her to breath and made her truly happy. In addition, since she was based out of the New York area, she was able to make the occasional trip back home and stay in close contact with friends and family.

***

Arlene Florence Albino:

Even as a young girl, Arlene Albino always had, "a real bug for traveling." Growing up in Lyndhurst and Rutherford, New Jersey, she recalls, "the thrill," of having the opportunity to fly with her father and uncle in her uncle's small private plane. At the age of nineteen, having earned an associate's degree, but lacking the money required to continuing her education, Arlene was at a crossroads. She can't recall all these years later who it was, but someone, friend or relative, suggested that she might pursue a career as a flight attendant. Although the prospect of working in the airline industry and traveling for a living certainly appealed to her on some level, Arlene was more of an intellectual. She was an excellent student from a blue-collar Italian family that simply couldn't afford to continue paying their youngest daughter's tuition. If she couldn't go to school, Arlene decided that becoming a flight attendant, where she could earn a living, albeit a very modest one, while having the opportunity to travel, was probably her best option. She was hired by Eastern Airlines and completed her training in October 1968, four months shy of her twentieth birthday.

Arlene described conversations with my dad as pleasant and professional. "I saw Captain Wilbur as this handsome older man. He was movie star handsome, and he carried himself in a reserved and dignified way, but without being unfriendly or unapproachable. . . . He wasn't a player, he didn't flirt or act inappropriately with the flight attendants like a lot of the other pilots did. I mean, we practically had to beat some of them off with a stick."

Arlene Albino was just twenty-two years old at the time of the hijacking and was still living with her parents in Rutherford. She had been flying the Newark-Washington and Newark-Boston shuttle, and had worked with my father on several previous occasions.

***

Sandra Kay Saltzer:

Sandra Saltzer was born and raised in the Rochester area of upstate New York. The eldest of four children by a wide margin, Sandy would have the luxury of being a kid, with the unfettered freedom to pursue her own interests above all others, until the ripe old age of ten. It would represent the only time in her life where she could truly, and exclusively, indulge in thoughts of self. When siblings Mark, Caroline, and Anne Marie came along, Sandy was thrust into the role of caregiver to her younger brother and sisters. Her two working parents, Robert Saltzer, a teacher, and Margaret Saltzer, a court clerk, depended on her a great deal, not only to jump in and help with chores and the like, but to be a mentor and secondary parent in their absence. Though difficult at times, Sandy didn't shy away from this responsibility, she embraced it.

Over time, and from a very young age, Sandy developed into a strong, caring, and nurturing individual. She became so comfortable and at ease in this role, and the required skills and demeanor became so entrenched in her, that, for Sandy, it became a life's pursuit. Circumstances would, however, cause an interesting and lengthy detour in the career path of this woman, who, in her heart of hearts has always been a caregiver.

In 1966, Sandy earned her bachelor's degree in nursing from SUNY Plattsburgh. Her two college roommates, also nursing majors, were from Long Island and Staten Island, New York, and were both able to secure work back home in area hospitals after graduation. Sandy decided to join them. She moved to Long Island where the three friends shared an apartment. Sandy found work at a local school as a school nurse teacher (SNT), and worked at Good Samaritan Hospital in West Islip during the summer months.

Two years out of college, and all three with steady paying jobs, the roommates decided to take a trip to Europe. They spent a month touring Germany, Austria, Italy, and other places Sandy can't quite recall. It was Sandy's second time on an airplane, and her first extended vacation, and she absolutely fell in love with traveling. And it wasn't just the being there, in the new, beautiful, interesting, and exciting places that appealed to her, it was also the getting there. Sandy loved to fly. It just so happened that shortly after her return home from Europe, on her twenty-third birthday, at a party in Patchogue, Long Island, single and unattached, Sandy met a young pilot working for Northwest Airlines. George was also twenty-three, and coincidentally, it was his birthday too. The two found each other interesting enough and they ended up dating for several years. Getting to know Sandy, and learning about her newfound love of travel, George suggested she take a leave of absence from nursing and take a stab at becoming a flight attendant. Being young, and just recently back from her month-long European adventure, and with the influence of a new love interest, she decided to give it a go.

Sandy applied to several airlines, including Northwest, and was ultimately hired by Eastern in August of 1969.

7. The Hijacking

Having completed her six weeks of training by late September 1969, Sandy Saltzer had less than six months on the job when she was confronted with a gun wielding passenger on March 17, 1970, aboard Eastern Airlines Flight 1320. She was collecting fares on the short flight from Newark Airport to Logan International with Senior Flight Attendant Christine Peterson and it was all going by the numbers, until she approached the man in seat 22D. Other than the fact that he was wearing sunglasses at night, Sandy didn't think there was anything particularly noticeable or peculiar about John Joseph Divivo, Jr.

"When I asked him for his fare he said he was a student and handed me eighteen dollars, which was the student rate at that time. When I asked him for some kind of student identification he took out a gun from what looked like a shaving kit. He said he wanted to see the captain, but I told him I couldn't do that. He pointed the gun at me without really extending his arm that much, probably still trying to keep it somewhat concealed. He said, 'I'm not joking, I want to see the captain.' I told him that I'd take him to the cockpit, but I asked him to put away the gun, so he wouldn't scare the other passengers. He put the gun in his coat pocket and I walked him to the front of the plane."

Christine Peterson followed the two to the front of the aircraft and remained there until the conclusion of the flight, ready to assist in any way possible.

Peggy McLoughlin was a nineteen-year-old sophomore at Boston College, returning to school after spending spring break at home in Livingston, New Jersey, with her parents. The second-year special education major had traveled to and from school on the Eastern Shuttle before, and the trip had always been uneventful. Peggy was on the left side of the plane and approximately five or six rows back. She saw a flight attendant walk past her seat on her way to the cockpit accompanied by a man walking closely behind. The man had what looked to be a small bag in his hand.

Emanuel Abrams was hurrying home to his wife, Barbara, and daughters Zoe and Katy after a business trip the New York/New Jersey area. Manny was a forty-six-year-old self-employed business consultant who lived in the town of Natick, Massachusetts. Seated on the left side of the plane, approximately two-thirds of the way back, Manny was reading *Time* Magazine when he too saw a flight attendant heading up to the front of the plane with a man walking right behind her.

At approximately 8:00 p.m., Flight 1320 was between twenty-five and thirty nautical miles southwest of the Boston VORTAC at an altitude of five thousand five hundred feet and nearing its destination when Flight Attendant Sandy Saltzer rang the flight deck and informed the captain that a passenger wanted to speak with him. Both pilots were extremely busy during this stage of the flight, and the captain told Sandy that the passenger would have to wait until they were safely on the ground. After Sandy explained that the passenger was armed, co-pilot Jim Hartley opened the cockpit door and allowed John Joseph Divivo, Jr. to enter, along with Sandy. The .38 caliber revolver that Divivo held in his right hand made for a suitably compelling argument to allow his entry. Remember, this wasn't exactly a post-9/11 environment. Circa 1970, hijackings, although not exactly common place, weren't extremely rare either, and standard operating procedure was to cooperate.

Sandy asked if there was anything she could do, and Captain Wilbur replied, "No, you better go and take care of the passengers." She left the cockpit and closed the door behind her.

The dimmer lighting in the cockpit must have made it necessary for Divivo to remove his sunglasses which, according to eyewitness testimony, had remained on for the entire flight up to that point. To this day my father still remembers the strange look on his face. It wasn't quite a smile, but more of a smirk. The eyes were anxious and alert, with a hint of crazy, but were simultaneously lifeless and resigned. His rather dull affect could almost be characterized as lethargic, and it was off-putting, and more than a bit confusing, as it didn't match the gravity of the situation.

"Man, I don't know what's wrong. I'm all fucked up," he said as he pointed the gun toward both pilots.

The captain and first officer did their best to try to deescalate the situation. They offered Divivo the jump-seat and made casual conversation in an effort to keep him calm. He continued to say odd things like, "I don't know what's wrong with me," and the statements seemed to be directed as much to himself as to the pilots, which made it pretty clear he was more than a bit off. Divivo asked them where they were going, as if he didn't already know, and they told him, "Boston." He said that he didn't want to go to Boston, and the captain asked him where he did want to go.

At that point Jim Hartley casually squawked 3100 on the plane's transponder to alert air traffic control that the plane was being hijacked. Today's aircraft use transponder code 7500 to alert controllers of a hijacking. Air traffic control had already instructed First Officer Hartley to change over to the Boston approach control frequency.

Flight 1320 had been cleared to descend to fifteen hundred feet and was given vector 080° for landing on runway 27. This left traffic pattern for runway 27 would mean that, from south of the airport, the plane was to fly an easterly heading of 080°, followed by a left turn to a heading of 360°, followed by another left turn for a final approach heading of 270°.

Divivo told Captain Wilbur that he wanted to fly east but wouldn't specify any particular destination. When the captain explained that the DC-9 they were flying wasn't carrying a heck of a lot of fuel for the short flight, Divivo replied, "Let me know when we're two minutes from running out of fuel." When Boston approach instructed Flight 1320, which was now flying a heading of 080° at an altitude of fifteen hundred feet, to turn left to a heading of 360°, Jim Hartley, who was tasked with handling radio communications during this leg of the trip, asked for permission to break out of the traffic pattern and continue heading east.

First Officer Hartley: Eastern 1320, we're gonna take up a heading of east here for a while and go out over the water.
Approach: Do you have a problem?
First Officer Hartley: Affirmed.
Approach: Turn right heading zero…ah….provide your own navigation sir and…ah..you'll be at fifteen hundred?
First Officer Hartley: Yes, we'll stay at fifteen hundred, 1320.
Approach: I want you to advise me when you intend to proceed inbound, we have numerous aircraft on deck.

Flight 1320 had already squawked 3100 on its transponder which should have alerted ATC of the hijacking, however it appears that they were somehow unaware. Later radio transmissions confirm that air traffic controllers were confused as to which aircraft in the traffic pattern was under duress.

Following the mad man's instructions would certainly have doomed the flight and killed all seventy-three passengers and crew aboard the aircraft, and neither pilot could allow that. After continuing on an easterly heading over the Atlantic Ocean for another five miles or so, Captain Wilbur asked if it would be alright if he turned back. Divivo simply replied, "Yeah, it's okay."

Approach: Eastern 1320 are you still at fifteen hundred?
First Officer Hartley: (After a 17 second delay) Eastern 1320, we're ah, we're heading back in now, you have a heading you want us to fly?

Captain Wilbur looked left to clear the plane for its turn back toward Logan Airport. Just as he began to make the turn, an ear shattering explosion filled the cockpit. He spun to his right just in time to catch a glimpse of the black barreled, smoking, .38 caliber revolver pointing at him. He doesn't recall raising his right arm in a futile attempt to try to stave off the inevitable, but the simple laws of physics, along with forensic evidence, make it a certainty. Another deafening explosion was followed by the excruciating pain and burning, as a single bullet tore through his right forearm and into his upper left bicep, shattering bone. Just one more pull of the trigger would certainly have meant the end, however, in that instant, something truly extraordinary happened. Despite having been shot in the back at point blank range, First Officer Jim Hartley spun in his seat and lunged toward the hijacker, grabbing his gun. A stunned John Divivo was quickly overpowered by the first officer whose incredible display of guts and determination saved the life of his captain, and in so doing, gave the other passengers and crew of Flight 1320 a fighting chance to survive. Jim Hartley managed to shoot the hijacker twice in their brief struggle, before slumping in his seat and dropping the gun on the center console between he and the captain. Divivo dropped to the cockpit floor. He was down, but not out. The cockpit of a DC-9-31 had roughly the same square footage as a small SUV, minus the trunk, and with enough headroom to stand. Imagine for a moment what a gun battle in your Ford Escape might be like. Imagine your ears ringing while you struggle to get a clean breath through the smoke caused by the detonation of gun powder. Imagine your heart pounding in your chest to a degree you've never felt before, simultaneously fraying your nerves, while expelling blood from your body at an alarming rate.

The captain, now bleeding profusely from gunshot wounds to both arms, and with his first officer, his friend, three feet to his right, now completely immobile and dying of his own gunshot wound, was tasked with landing his aircraft. All of this with a mentally disturbed, suicidal hijacker on the floor, still conscious and still motivated to end his own life, along with the lives of every other soul onboard.

The gun battle and physical struggle in the confined area had caused the cockpit door to fly open. Flight attendants Sandy Saltzer and Christine Peterson, as well as the passengers near the front of the aircraft, could now see the results of the carnage within. The captain picked up the .38 and placed it on the dashboard near the nose wheel steering wheel to his left. John Divivo was lying on the floor of the cockpit with his legs now protruding out into the cabin. The captain recalls him saying something like, "I can't even die."

When the shooting started, Arlene Albino, who was sitting in the jump seat in the rear of the plane, felt an immediate and precipitous drop in altitude, followed by a steady, but scary-fast decent. At some point she moved up to the middle area of the plane and sat in a passenger seat. She thought they were all going to die and was praying and thinking about all the things she'd never get to experience, like getting married and having children. Arlene half smiled when she recalled her sense of dread at seeing the "Fasten Seatbelt" sign light up. "I thought to myself, this is the end, and I thought we were crashing. I thought, this is the ultimate irony, this guy is putting the seatbelt sign on just to mess with us, and when we actually landed, I mean, there was nobody more surprised than me."

Hearing the gunshots, Sandy more than considered the possibility that she would never leave the aircraft alive. She doesn't recall her life flashing before her eyes, nor does she remember having any particular thoughts of loss or remorse over a life cut short. Unlike Arlene, whose relief came only after she felt the plane touch down on the runway, Sandy could clearly see into the cockpit after its door was blown open by the gunshot and by the force of the struggle within. She recalls seeing Captain Wilbur conscious and at the controls of the airplane. Although she could see that he was bleeding and that he was seriously injured, he had a calmness and control about him that told her everything would be alright.

Peggy McLoughlin heard questions making the rounds in the cabin: "Is there a doctor on board?" "Is there a pilot on board?" At nineteen Peggy lacked the maturity and awareness to understand the gravity of the situation. She debated whether to take her boots off in case of a water landing, thinking that she'd be able to swim better in her bare feet.

Captain Wilbur turned west toward Logan Airport, raised flaps, which had been engaged at 5°, and increased his speed to 250 knots (288 miles per hour). He radioed Boston approach and informed them that his first officer had been shot and was unconscious, and that they needed to be cleared for an immediate landing.

Approach: Eastern 1320, ah, you squawking VFR [Visual Flight Rules] now?
Captain Robert Wilbur: Negative, we're on 3100 and you better get the police to the airport, we just had, ah, the co-pilot is shot.

This statement, preserved on the cockpit recording, is by far the most emotion I've ever heard in my father's voice. The emotion I heard, however, falls well short of the horror and panic one might expect from anyone faced with a similar ordeal. It was typical of my father, and just the type of cool-headed response the impossible situation called for. It's difficult to describe, but on a distress level scale of 1 to 10, his subsequent transmissions sounded like someone at about a 4. He sounded like a pilot who was a bit low on fuel and didn't want to waste any time getting his plane on the ground.

Captain Wilbur: (After a five second delay and no response from Boston approach) Get us in in a hurry Bos.
Approach: 1320, I got you, continue right inbound to the airport, you're thirteen miles, ident. on code 04.
Captain Wilbur: Get an ambulance to the airport also.
Approach: Yes Sir, we're alerting all the equipment, continue, you're right inbound now you're on a twelve-mile final for runway 27. There is traffic at 12, 11:30 and five miles ahead of you, and it's an, ah, Mohawk Bac-111.
Captain Wilbur: Okay, get a doctor there, quick.
Approach: (Thirty-eight seconds later) Eastern 1320, what is your airspeed please?
Captain Wilbur: 250.
Approach: Alright sir, thanks.

Approach: (Forty-six seconds later) Eastern 1320, you're on a six-mile final, that Mohawk aircraft is about three and a half miles ahead of you sir.

The absurdity of this last transmission, and what it meant, can't possibly be overstated, and highlights the inexplicably blah-zee attitude of the controller, given what was unfolding. In just under a minute and a half, from the time Boston approach control called Eastern Airlines Flight 1320 on a twelve-mile final, the aircraft had cut the distance in half. It was now six miles out, in an emergency situation, with its first officer shot and seriously injured, traveling at 250 knots, and crawling up the ass of a smaller, slower aircraft, yet controllers had still not cleared a path.

Captain Wilbur: Okay. (Eight seconds later) We're comin' on in.

Flight 1320 was approximately thirteen miles east of Logan when the captain began his lightning push toward the airport. Now, if you will, climb back into your SUV and imagine being carjacked at night on a deserted road thirteen miles from home. You've been shot in both arms, and are bleeding out, and your friend has been shot and is dying right next to you. Your carjacker has also been shot, but is still conscious, and lying in the back seat. Now what if your small SUV were somehow able to tow a compartment filled with seventy other people whom you were responsible for. Would you be able to keep it together and somehow get home, or would the fear, the pain, the emotion, the overwhelming responsibility of the situation cause you to panic, to crumble? Remember, this was no car. It was an airplane with a gross weight of roughly 95,000 pounds, and it was being flown at a ridiculous speed in an effort to save Jim Hartley. The normal landing speed of a Douglas DC-9-31 was between 120 and 135 knots, depending on weight. Flight 1320 was traveling twice that speed.

My father was very well trained, no doubt. His time as a military pilot, with the repetition of thousands of hours of flight time, prepared him for virtually any emergency situation in an aircraft. But what training could possibly have prepared him for what he and Jim Hartley faced that night? Although military trained, he was never a combat soldier, and over the years when I asked him how? why? he was able to respond to the hijacking the way he did, he could offer nothing in the way of self-analysis. I eventually came to realize that, in addition to his detached, almost icy demeanor, the result, I believe, of both nature and nurture, he simply fell back on what he knew, and he certainly knew how to fly. Pilots are trained to follow a checklist, and he did so, to the letter, even turning on the "Fasten Seatbelt" sign. A fact that would one day become good fodder for his pilot buddies when talking about the incident in years to come.

Eastern Airlines Flight 1320 was cleared for landing on runway 27. For reasons unknown, air traffic control neglected to instruct other approaching aircraft to clear a path. A small twin engine Mohawk was nearly run down and was given an almost too late instruction by ATC to execute a missed approach. From thirteen miles out, and flying at a dangerously high speed, Flight 1320 was on the ground in just under four minutes. However, with the plane just two to three miles from its destination, hijacker John Divivo, decided he needed to do more than just mutter to himself about another failed suicide attempt. Likely feeling the energy and the adrenaline ebbing from his body and seeing that the captain was now focused solely on landing the aircraft, Divivo probably thought it was now or never, and he began to stir. He got to his knees, grabbing and clawing at the captain. Captain Wilbur managed to grab the black .38 caliber revolver from the dashboard in front of him with his left hand, a hand attached to an arm which was home to a .38 caliber slug, transfer it to his right hand, a hand attached to a forearm which was torn apart by the same .38 caliber slug, and repeatedly smash it over the hijacker's head, causing the handle of the gun to break apart into four pieces.

Mary Armstead from Winston-Salem, North Carolina, was in the fifth row on the right side of the plane. "I saw the pilot hitting the man while he was lying on his back with some object. The assailant then yelled, 'I want to die, I want to die.'" Steven Jeffries from Greensboro, North Carolina, was in the fourth row on the left side. "The pilot was partially out of his seat and struggling with the assailant. The co-pilot was lying over one arm of his seat and a lot of blood was visible on the captain's right and left arms." Bart Collins, also from Greensboro, North Carolina, was seated in the third-row window seat on the left side of the plane. "I saw blood on both arms and the lower back of the pilot as his coat was off, and the blood was very visible through his white shirt."

Divivo once again slumped to the floor, allowing the captain to turn his attention to the all-important final moments of the flight.

My father has never been able to adequately describe the pain or the fear he must have felt, nor why he simply didn't put a bullet in Divivo's head. To the latter he has always said, without any meaningful elaboration, "I just couldn't do that." As to the former, the adrenaline rush he must have experienced would have lasted less than a minute and, in my mind, doesn't come close to explaining how he was able to do what he did.

Captain Wilbur later gave the following report of the incident to Eastern Airline Chief Pilot, Captain W.R. Krepling. His cool, detailed description of Flight 1320's final approach reads as if a robot had been at the controls. His offhanded, almost afterthought inclusion of the hijacker's attempt to menace the flight in its final moments, and his subsequent response, demonstrate the lengths to which he went to portray his actions as ordinary, thereby downplaying his own heroism:

"We were cleared directly in for a landing on runway 27 with mileage being given by approach control with each radio transmission. We had the 266° radial of Boston VORTAC turned into our OMNI beaming selector, which is the runway 27 instrument approach radial to be followed. A Mohawk flight was instructed to go around as we approached the runway. At approximately five miles from the end of the runway, (roughly 3 miles out) the landing gear was lowered, flaps were lowered, the spoilers were armed, and the seatbelt sign turned on. Shortly before landing we were told to change over to the tower frequency and a normal landing was made. I should mention that at approximately two miles out on final approach, the gunman tried to get up off the floor. I took the gun from in front of the nose wheel steering wheel with my left hand, transferred it to my right hand, and hit the gunman with the flat side of the gun on top of the head. We made our landing on runway 27 and taxied off the runway at taxiway Sierra."

Eastern 1320 was safely on the ground one minute and five seconds after the captain told Logan Tower, "1320's comin' in."

Tower: (After landing) Eastern 1320 any right turn as soon as you're ready, taxi right to the gate.
Captain Wilbur: Okay, my co-pilot is discombobulated here, he can't talk or anything, he's passed out. ***We've been shot.***

The plane is now safely on the ground and this is the very first time that the captain informs an air traffic controller that he's been shot! When asked about it over the years, his explanation has been simple and consistent. He was extremely busy flying the airplane and didn't see the importance of mentioning it. He made sure to convey the gravity of the situation in order to expedite their arrival at Logan Airport, and he, of course, wanted to make certain that medical personnel, and police, would be there to meet the plane. He knew Jim was in really bad shape and wanted to get to Logan as fast as possible to give him a fighting chance. Is it possible that he never said the words out loud because doing so would have meant admitting to himself that he'd been shot and was seriously hurt? Would that acknowledgment have somehow weakened his resolve, making him realize just how impossible his situation was? Did his refusal to acknowledge his own terrible injuries somehow allow him to find the strength to do what only the rarest of men would have been capable of?

***

As the plane taxied to Gate 12 at Logan International, Arlene worked her way to the front of the plane. "I remember one woman grabbing, and hugging me, and crying…I remember oddly thinking that I should say something like, 'Welcome to Boston,' or 'Thank you for flying Eastern.'"

Senior Flight Attendant Christine Peterson opened the aircraft door and a ground crew attached a portable jetway. It was the old-school stairway kind that were still prevalent in 1970. Logan had recently completed a large renovation of its terminals which included modern style jetways like the ones used at today's airports. Speed, however, was of the essence, and emergency personnel and law enforcement could more quickly and easily access the aircraft right from the tarmac.

Three Massachusetts State Troopers sprinted up the jetway stairs and forcibly removed a now fully conscious John Divivo from the floor of the cockpit as he struggled, and fought, and clung to whatever he could grab on to in an effort to remain on the airplane. Now at the front of the plane, Arlene saw the aftermath of the shooting. "A few police officers were dragging the hijacker, who was still kicking and fighting, out of the plane and down the stairs." Passenger Mike Clover remembers, "The state troopers boarded the plane and fought heavily with the assailant to remove him."

"The next thing I saw was the captain standing in the doorway with blood all over him," Arlene continued. "He stepped back and told the officers, 'I'm fine, take care of my co-pilot.' The officers carried Jim Hartley out of the plane, down the stairs, and into a waiting ambulance. Captain Wilbur followed him out."

Paramedics quickly, but gently, lifted Jim Hartley from his co-pilot seat, placed him on a stretcher, and carried him down the jetway stairs into a waiting ambulance. He was completely unresponsive. This was all in clear view of the captain who was now standing just outside of the blood-stained cockpit.

Passenger Manny Abrams was able to maneuver a bit closer to the front of the cabin and recalls seeing police officers carry the unconscious co-pilot from the cockpit. Passengers erupted in applause as the captain emerged a moment later. The captain stood at the precipice of the exit door, a stoic and concerned look on his face. From Manny's vantage point, it appeared that the captain was simply watching to make sure his friend was handled with care. A great deal of blood was clearly visible on both of his shirt sleeves, but the captain never wavered. He disappeared down the jetway, and Manny never saw him again.

Captain Wilbur followed his first officer down the jetway stairs and sat down on the second to last step, watching, hoping. When the door to Jim's ambulance closed, he took a deep breath and put his head in his hands. Asking him what he was thinking, or how he was feeling, at that precise moment has been an exercise in futility. However, knowing him as I do, I'd say that he was likely running the chain of events over and over in his mind, picking apart every detail, trying to figure out what went wrong. What could he have done differently that might have produced a different outcome? One that didn't include the likely death of his first officer and friend. In the moments that followed, as he waited to be escorted into his own ambulance, as the adrenaline ebbed, and the shock of the traumatic event started to settle in, he began to feel the full impact of his own injuries and was grateful to be alive. John Joseph Divivo, Jr., had failed for a second time to end his own life, and in so doing, he lost the battle to end the lives of so many others. All three men were rushed to Massachusetts General Hospital.

After deplaning Manny Abrams was taken to a room with other passengers and questioned by the authorities. He remembers being offered a shot of Chivas Regal, which he gladly accepted. There was a brief press interview, an emotional call to his family, and a car ride home to Natick, Massachusetts. Manny had done his best to keep his emotions in check, but while driving home he began shaking uncontrollably and had to pull over on the Mass Pike to calm himself down.

At Mass General First Officer James E. Hartley, Jr. was pronounced dead on arrival at 8:35 p.m. He was just thirty years old.

8. On the Ground

One of Eastern's chief pilots, Captain John O'Neil, was sitting at home when he got the call from a high-level Eastern executive. He was briefed in as much detail as was available on the incident and was charged with the task of notifying the captain's wife and arranging for her transport up to Boston. He thought about how best to accomplish the task and decided the employ the services of two local captains whom he thought might be able to deliver the news in as delicate a manner as possible. The plan was that one of the two men would remain with my mother and accompany her to Boston, as she was sure to be more than a bit shaken by the news, and no doubt frightened out of her skin.

When he rang the doorbell to our small three-bedroom cape in Fair Lawn, Captain Murray E. (Buddy) Burke was greeted by my grandmother who ushered him inside. My mother was just wrapping up a very brief, but nonetheless disconcerting phone call she received from a man who identified himself as a reporter from California. The man asked her if she was the wife of Captain Robert Wilbur, "The pilot whose plane was hijacked." She signaled my grandmother to turn on the television, and the story was front and center. They identified my father by name, but the stock photo that was used wasn't him. This gave my mother a glimmer of hope until she saw Buddy Burke standing in our living room. Buddy told her that my dad's plane had been hijacked, and that he was injured, and they needed to get to Boston. Buddy Burke was a Marine Corp. veteran who was hired by Eastern in 1957. He lived close by in Montvale, and he and my dad had flown together on occasion over the years, which made him a reasonable candidate for the assignment. Another area captain, Bob Alexander, also known to my father, had a reputation as a light-hearted, fun-loving guy, whom everyone liked. He came to the house as well, and was a logical choice to lighten the mood, and, if for no other reason, was there for added comfort and solidarity.

Eastern Airlines First Officer J.P. Tristani was sitting at home watching TV when news of the hijacking broke. Although the name didn't jibe with the face plastered across his television, his heart sank because he knew the flight, and was almost certain that it was my father's plane that had been hijacked. He and his wife, Reggie, also lived in Fair Lawn, just a short distance away, and they immediately made their way to our house. When they stepped inside they saw that a number of Eastern executives, along with Buddy Burke and Bob Alexander, were already there. This was 1970, and the house probably looked a bit like the TV series *Mad Men*. There were a bunch of men, mostly in suits, puffing away on cigarettes and engaged in serious conversation.

My mom was busy packing for the trip. She was clearly in shock and unable to focus on the task at hand. She was running around in circles haphazardly pulling clothes out of drawers and putting them back, taking shoes out of closets, searching in vain for things she'd put her hands on a thousand times before, but was now somehow unable to find. When she saw J.P. and Reggie, she stopped short, and the three engaged in a group hug that lingered for a long time. This prompted my mother to break down for the first time. Reggie insisted on accompanying her to Boston, and she and J.P. ran back home to pack her a bag. As I said, J.P. and Reggie lived close by and had been family friends for years. They should have been first on the scene, but J.P. wasn't a captain, and I suppose among Eastern management common sense was trumped by their ridged protocols.

My four-year-old sister, Allison, was wide awake when the phone started to ring and serious-looking people began to arrive at the house. She was a bundle of energy and not always the best sleeper. I was sound asleep like a grizzly bear in the dead of winter, apparently a very typical state for me. Before leaving for the airport, my mom snuck into my bedroom and kissed me on the cheek as I slept. She hugged and kissed Allison, never wanting to let go, but knowing she had to. She was able to draw strength in the knowledge that she was leaving her two precious gems in the very capable hands of her mother, affectionately known to us as GaGa.

No matter her appearance as a younger woman, I always knew my grandmother, Mary Decicco, as a stout five foot five and just about the sweetest woman I've ever known. She was an amazing cook and an even better story teller, who could routinely make her audience, along with herself, laugh until she, and they, cried. Gogs, as my sister and I came to call her, had the unique ability to water down any problem with just a kind word or stroke of her hand. The timing of her week-long visit couldn't have been better, and she steadfastly took charge of the household allowing my mother to face the emotional roller-coaster that lay ahead.

Buddy Burke called JFK crew-scheduling and arranged for passes to be waiting for my mom, Reggie, and Bob Alexander on the last shuttle flight out from Newark to Boston that night. J.P. had given Bob a nice bottle of Remy Cognac to be used for medicinal purposes on the flight, and I'm told he drank most of it himself. Buddy would chauffer the three from our house in Fair Lawn to Newark Airport. The car ride and short flight to Boston was the longest and most excruciating two hours of my mother's life. The time passed with very little conversation taking place, even between my mom and Reggie, save for the occasional comforting platitudes one would expect given the situation. It was the uncertainty that was killing her, and there wasn't anything anyone could do or say that might dissuade her from the feeling that her whole world might soon fall apart.

When their DC-9 landed at Logan International, it was met by an Eastern employee whose job it was to escort VIPs to and from the airport. Stephen Fowler began his career with Eastern Airlines as a part-time gate agent in July 1968, a few months after returning home from Vietnam following his three-year stint in the Marine Corps. In 1969, he applied for and got a full-time position as an Executive Service Representative, working at Eastern's downtown Boston sales office. He was a young man, less than two years removed from a grueling military service, with a young wife and newborn baby. Stephen was happy to have caught on with Eastern Airlines full-time, and he like his job. Driving high-level Eastern executives, and the occasional celebrity, in a plush limousine had to be considered light duty to the Marine, and he appreciated the opportunity to meet new and interesting people. He routinely drove Eastern's president, Floyd Hall, and vice president (later president) Sam Higginbottom, and too many celebrities to count. He was particularly thrilled when he picked up Johnny Cash at the airport one night and drove him to his hotel. He was in Boston for a concert, which Stephen happened to have tickets to.

On the night of March 17, 1970, Stephen remembers being at home with his wife and newborn when the phone rang. It was his boss, Loren Cain, who never called him at home. In fact, he rarely heard from Loren at all, unless there was a problem. Stephen always got his assignments from the reservation agents at Eastern's Executive Services office in Woodbridge, New Jersey, so when he picked up the phone and heard his boss's voice, his first thought was that he'd done something to piss the man off. Loren asked him if he'd been watching the news, to which he stammered, "No." His boss told him that an Eastern Shuttle from Newark to Logan had been hijacked and that both pilots were shot. He needed to get to the airport ASAP to pick up the captain's wife and take her to Mass General. He was specifically instructed to avoid any press that might be hovering around the hospital, but Loren reiterated that he should get her there fast because they had no idea how badly the captain was hurt.

Stephen arrived in time to meet the flight at Logan's newly renovated shuttle gates and spirited his three passengers away with all speed. In sparse traffic, Massachusetts General Hospital is about a twelve- to fifteen-minute ride from the airport. Stephen got them there in just under ten. He was able to pull right up in front of the main doors, as there wasn't yet a press van or microphone in sight. He parked the car and remained with his passengers for a brief period, after which he was given the green light to go home.

"As I think back on it now," Stephen told me, "your mom, given that she was the wife of Captain Wilbur, was the most important person I ever transported in my career."

My father was in surgery when my mom arrived at the hospital. She and her companions were ushered to a waiting room where they were able to sit in relative quiet. When the press did arrive, they did so in earnest, but were kept at bay by Massachusetts State Police officers, who certainly made their presence known. Hospital staff spoke with my mother as did State Police investigators who were chomping at the bit to get the captain's statement. They said Captain Wilbur was in surgery and wouldn't be able to give a statement for at least forty-eight hours. At this point my mom's nerves were shot and her emotional state ran the gamut. She had learned that my father was shot in the arms and that the bullet had not struck any vital organs. No one, however, was willing to give her a definitive answer as the whether he would live or die. She had heard the awful news about their friend, Jim Hartley, which added to her grief and shrouded the situation with an additional layer of misery that was almost too much to bear. Understandably, she just couldn't sit still, and began pacing outside the operation room. She was accompanied by Reggie, and they were soon joined by a plain clothes police officer who appeared to be waiting for something.

***

Doctor Ashby C. Moncure, one of the on-call surgeons at Massachusetts General Hospital on the night of March 17, 1970, was told to prepare for the arrival of a thirty-five-year-old male who had suffered multiple gunshot wounds. A 1960 graduate of the University of Virginia School of Medicine, Dr. Moncure had worked at the very busy Mass General for a number of years and was a highly skilled trauma surgeon, specializing in cardiac, vascular, and thoracic surgery. He was about my father's age and had seen just about everything in his relatively young career. When my father arrived at the hospital he was conscious but less than alert. The EMTs had done their job in stemming the massive flow of blood and easing the pain of his wounds. He had, however, lost a great deal of blood and was immediately taken into surgery.

Doctor Moncure had seen worse in the time he'd spent as a trauma surgeon at Boston's busiest hospital. His concerns in my father's case were two-fold. First, the gaping hole created by the exiting of the .38 caliber bullet on the inside of his right forearm might have damaged tendons, possibly limiting the use of the right hand. The wound was so large that it would require multiple skin grafts to adequately close. The second delicate part of the surgery would be extracting the bullet fragments from his upper left bicep without damaging the arm. Doctor Moncure first worked on my dad's right arm, which had, thankfully, not sustained irreparable damage. He grafted skin from his left thigh to close the wound and would do so several more times over the course of the following three weeks. In the midst of operating on the left bicep, and with his patient now stable, Doctor Moncure left the operating room.

Just before beginning his surgery, the doctor has been approached by a plain clothes detective of the Massachusetts State Police, who had asked him to secure the bullet he would retrieve from Captain Wilbur's arm. As a trauma surgeon at a hospital like Mass General, this wasn't the doctor's first rodeo. He's certainly had police officers linger outside of his operating rooms before. He was told that the bullet was an important piece of evidence in a criminal investigation involving the murder of one man and the attempted murder of another. As he now approached that same detective, who was waiting outside the O.R., he saw a woman out of the corner of his eye making a bee line in his direction. Before he could utter a word, she cut between he and the detective, and through newly formed tears stammered, "Is my husband alright? Is he gonna be okay?" The doctor assured Mrs. Wilbur that her husband was out of the woods and would be just fine. He then gently turned his attention to the detective informing him that the bullet in his patient's left arm had fragmented into two pieces, and that only one of the two had been extracted. The other piece of lead had made its way into a sensitive area, and if they dug any further in an attempt to reach it, they ran the risk of permanently damaging the arm. My mom, who never made a move to leave the doctor's side, started to speak, but the detective made what she was about to say a moot point. He told Doctor Moncure to leave the remainder of the bullet where it was. They could certainly make their case without it.

***

One of Eastern's assistant chief pilots, Captain Paul Quigley, drew the unenviable assignment of placing a call to Becky Hartley at her home in Fort Lee, New Jersey.

He told her that her husband's plane had been hijacked and that Jim had been shot and seriously wounded. Becky was only in her mid-twenties, and she and Jim had been married less than a year. A transplanted Floridian, like her husband, she had no family in the area. Needless to say, she was ill-equipped to handle the news that awaited her.

Becky was picked up by an Eastern captain, whom she didn't know, and driven to the airport where she was put on a plane to Boston. Jim Hartley had been pronounced DOA long before his wife arrived at Mass General with her escort. She was told of his passing by Eastern personnel who were awaiting her arrival at the hospital. Becky was inconsolable. When she was finally able to compose herself she immediately left the hospital and was taken to a nearby hotel. The following day she was put on a plane back home and, with the assistance of Eastern Airlines management, began the awful task of arranging her husband's funeral, which would take place just outside his hometown of Miami, Florida.

9. The Prosecution

James Hartley's autopsy was performed by the Suffolk County Medical Examiner on March 18, 1970, at approximately 10:30 a.m. The medical examiner determined that he had been shot in the upper left area of his back. Powder residue indicated that he was shot at point blank range. The forensic examination of Hartley's body revealed that a single bullet entered the upper left portion of his back just below the shoulder blade, passed through the left lung and aorta fracturing a rib on the right side, and exiting at the right breast near the right armpit. This single devastating gunshot finally grazed the co-pilot's right bicep before coming to rest on the cockpit floor.

An examination of Hartley's left hand revealed powder residue in the vicinity of the index finger. This was certainly the result of his struggle with the hijacker and the subsequent shots fired. The medical examiner determined that Jim Hartley, "...could have lived only a few minutes after the wound was inflicted due to the large amount of blood found in the chest cavity as a result of the puncture of the aorta." I certainly don't claim to be an historian, but the circumstances surrounding Jim's death have always made me wonder. Has anyone in history done more in their final moments to save so many lives? I've always wondered something else. What would have happened if Divivo hadn't attempted suicide more than 11 years earlier? The bullet he lodged in his sixteen year old brain had caused permanent and debilitating injuries, including a loss of vision and the partial paralysis of his left side. Could a mortally wounded Jim Hartley have wrestled the gun away from a perfectly health twenty-seven year old John Joseph Divivo Jr.? I suppose we'll never know.

Captain Wilbur suffered gunshot wounds to both arms. A single .38 caliber bullet ripped through his right forearm before penetrating his left upper bicep, breaking the bone just below his shoulder. The bullet had fragmented and caused a great deal of damage. Doctors were only able to remove a portion of the metal in Captain Wilbur's arm, determining that further digging would have risked causing irreparable damage. Bullet fragments remain in his left bicep to this day, as do the large diamond shaped scares on both sides of his right forearm.

As for the hijacker, one bullet had entered John Divivo's chest, causing serious but non-life-threatening injuries. The second shot was a through and through, just nicking the liver before exiting his body. It had fragmented and traveled through the closed cockpit door of the DC-9-31, ultimately embedding in a plastic partition in the front section of the aircraft. Divivo's surgeon told investigators he would be physically unable to be interviewed until March 19, 1970.

The following quotes are excerpts from a Massachusetts State Police forensic report: "After photographs were taken of the entire inside of the aircraft's cockpit, an examination of the inside area revealed a quantity of blood all over the console, floor, and seats… the large volume of blood made obtaining latent finger prints impossible." This was of no real importance as it was very clear who was present in the cockpit. A medallion belonging to Divivo, found on the floor of the cockpit, was described as follows: "…brass in color with a five-pointed star in the center of a ring measuring one half inch in diameter (a pentagram), attached to a twenty-two-inch broken chain… the handle of the .38 caliber revolver was broken into 5 pieces on cockpit floor." The captain had obviously shattered the butt of the gun on Divivo's head while attempting to subdue him. "Examination of the gun verified that four cartridges had been discharged and two were live."

Although the perpetrator of the hijacking was never in doubt, law enforcement had to exercise due diligence in their investigative efforts, and in the aftermath of Eastern Airlines Flight 1320, there was certainly no shortage of enthusiasm in this regard. From the very beginning, almost as soon as the DC-9-31 touched down at Logan International Airport, there was a great deal of jurisdictional fighting between the Massachusetts State Police and the Federal Bureau of Investigation. John Joseph Divivo, Jr. was taken from the aircraft by state troopers, placed under arrest, and mirandized during his transport to Massachusetts General Hospital. Following surgery, he was placed under twenty-four-hour guard. The FBI was not contacted by local authorities, but they were made aware of the hijacking by the Federal Aviation Administration.

Massachusetts State Police initially refused to allow FBI investigators to examine any evidence that they had obtained. They also denied access to witnesses, including the captain and John Divivo. On the morning of March 18, 1970, Assistant United States Attorney Howard Letterman had a telephone conference with Suffolk County Assistant District Attorney John Murphy, who emphatically stated that the Massachusetts State Police were, "Pushing extremely hard," and planned to go forward with a prosecution of John J. Divivo, Jr. for murder. This, despite statements made by another, unnamed assistant district attorney, who advised state police to, "Hold off until jurisdiction is decided."

During their verbal joust, Assistant United States Attorney Letterman pointed out that the crime took place some twelve miles over the Atlantic Ocean and, therefore, outside of the state's jurisdiction. He further argued that First Officer James E. Hartley, Jr., while pronounced at Massachusetts General Hospital, had almost certainly died while in federal airspace. Mr. Letterman was not at all shy about pointing out the fact that the FBI normally handled crimes aboard aircraft, had extensive experience, far superior expertise, and would be better able to handle the potentially complex investigation.

Later that day, a federal complaint was quickly filed charging Divivo with Crime Aboard Aircraft–Murder, in violation of Title 49, United States Code, Section 1472k. A warrant was issued and was served as a detainer. It was handed to one of the state police detectives guarding Divivo at Mass. General. The charges would later be expanded to include all of Divivo's transgressions. However, if the FBI thought the county prosecutor would now go away quietly, they were sadly mistaken. Their move only seemed to steel ADA Murphy's resolve, and he refused to back off, obtaining a murder warrant in the District Court of East Boston, which covers Logan Airport. On March 25, 1970, John J. Divivo, Jr. was indicted for the murder of James E. Hartley, Jr. by the Suffolk County Grand Jury in Boston, Massachusetts. He was arraigned on April 9, 1970, and plead not guilty. The Honorable Alfred Mahoney ordered Divivo committed to Bridgewater State Psychiatric Hospital for a thirty-five-day observation period.

On April 14, 1970, the facts of the case, including the current status of the state level prosecution against Divivo, were discussed by United States Attorney Edward J. Lee and his team of investigators. Mr. Lee decided to defer arraigning Divivo on the federal charges, which now included Destruction of Aircraft or Motor Vehicle, Crime Aboard Aircraft–Murder, and Assault with a Deadly Weapon, until after completion of his observation period at Bridgewater. These charges carried the death penalty.

10. Time to Heal

Meanwhile, at Mass General Hospital's Baker Building in room 816, the captain was laid-up and recovering from his injuries, my mom and the ever-present Reggie Tristani by his side. I might have failed to mention that Reggie, in addition to being a rock solid and loyal family friend, was a beautiful woman with a dulcet British accent. She had the unique ability of knowing just what to say and how to say it, and she knew when to make her presence known, and when to blend into the background. The importance of her companionship and support can't be overstated, and the gratitude felt by my family could never really be adequately expressed. J.P. had a trip to Boston on March 19, and he dropped off additional clothes and supplies for both ladies. Neither, of course, had the foresight to think about packing for an extended stay before leaving for the hospital on March 17th in such a frenzied state.

The large gaping wound on my father's right forearm was highly susceptible to bacterial infections and needed to be closed with the help of several skin grafts. WebMd describes the procedure as, "Incredibly painful," and it was. In addition, the daily changing of his bandages, necessary to ward off infection, was, according to my mom, excruciating to watch, let alone experience. His description of the twenty-eight days he spent in the hospital has always been matter of fact and measured, and quite typical of my dad's personality. He would only go so far as to say, "It hurt like hell, but after a few weeks I wanted to get the hell out of there." He spoke with state police detectives from his hospital bed just two days following his surgery and eventually gave a statement to the FBI as well. Investigators needed very little from him as the case was pretty cut and dried. For the most part, they kept their distance, save for the state police guards stationed in the hallway outside his room. The reason, or reasons, for their presence is a matter of opinion and is certainly open to debate. I believe they were there for one or more of the following: 1. To protect my father from John J. Divivo, Jr., who was only one floor above him and under round the clock police guard. He was not discharged from the hospital until April 9, 1970; 2. To keep out unwanted visitors, particularly press; 3. To keep out unwanted visitors, particularly the FBI, whom the state police were in a heated turf war with; 4. On the request of Eastern Airlines executives to keep out media in order to suppress a story that they'd just as soon see disappear.

The press was all over the story, but this was 1970, not 2019. There was no twenty-four hour news cycle, no TMZ. Journalists were so much fewer in number, and they weren't quite as aggressive in their approach to securing a story as they are today. That's not to say that there weren't attempts made by members of the press to penetrate the shield around my father. A few posed as family members, or Eastern personnel, to try to gain access. Eastern knew that the media wouldn't be kept at bay indefinitely, and their thinking, I believe, was that the longer they were kept waiting for their story, the bigger it would be, and that certainly wasn't in the company's best interest. They urged my mother to open herself up to a few questions during a brief press conference on the night of March 18. She specifically recalls a guy from California who asked the question, "Do you want your husband to quit flying?" Now it's important to keep in mind that, for the first couple of days, my mom was an absolute wreck. Her nerves were fried, she was still in shock, and doctors had put her on a valium regimen in an effort to help keep her from unraveling. Her simple response left the man speechless. She said, "We need pilots. If they all quit, how would you get here?"

A good number of visitors were, in fact, granted access to the hero captain of Flight 1320. Most of the Boston Bruins came for a brief visit, as did former astronaut and eventual chairman of Eastern Airlines, Frank Borman. Head of the F.A.A., John H. Shaffer, and former two-term Massachusetts governor and current (in 1970) U.S. Secretary of Transportation, John A. Volpe, paid a simultaneous visit and posed for a photo. My grandmother, Else Greene Wilbur, even took the time to fly up from Florida to see her boy. My grandfather stayed at home. My father's list of visitors was so large in number that the hospital offered to move him to a VIP floor where he would be put in a much larger suite and have exclusive access to several rooms. He declined, saying that he liked his nurse, a woman described by my mother as, "Not particularly nice or attentive."

In addition to visitors, phone calls came in by the dozens, not only from friends and family, but from politicians, sports stars, and actors, all wanting to congratulate him for what he'd done. He remembers taking a call from President Nixon who told him that his nation was proud of him and ever so grateful for his incredible bravery and skill, or something to that effect.

Martha Raye called him one day just to say how much she admired his courage under fire. Being unfamiliar with the name, I looked her up on Wikipedia and learned that she was an actress, singer, and comedian who was often thought of as the female Bob Hope for her extensive work with the USO. She was awarded the Presidential Medal of Freedom by President Clinton in 1993. The citation reads in part: "The great courage, kindness, and patriotism she showed in her many tours during World War II, the Korean conflict, and the Vietnam conflict earned her the nickname, 'Colonel Maggie'." Upon her death in 1994, she was buried with full military honors in the Fort Bragg post cemetery as an honorary colonel in the U.S. Marines and an honorary lieutenant colonel in the U.S. Army. According to Wikipedia, she is the one and only civilian buried at this location who receives military honors each Veterans Day.

That's pretty cool. Martha certainly had immense respect for the military and the feeling was obviously mutual. I suppose it's not a stretch to speculate that she may have taken a special interest in the hijacking given that both pilots were former military men.

My dad was, of course, lauded by everyone who came in contact with him, and he met each kind word with a polite, but ever modest, thank you. On those occasions when he was put in the uncomfortable position of continuing the conversation for any length of time, he would always deflect, and say that he was only doing his job, and that his co-pilot, Jim Hartley, was the real hero.

***

Jim's funeral mass was held at Philbrick Coral Gables Chapel in Coral Gables, Florida, at 3:00 p.m. on Friday March 20, 1970, less than seventy-two hours after the hijacking. Given the extent of his injuries, my father was not able to attend. It could be that this circumstance robbed him of much needed closure, adding to his angst and guilt over Jim's death. To this query his basic response has always been, "Bullshit." Psychoanalysis of a man like my father is a difficult if not impossible task, try as I may. J.P. took Reggie and my mom to Logan Airport and the three flew down together. The funeral was attended by every high-level Eastern executive from the chairman on down, as well as, the lion's share of every pilot in the company who wasn't in the air. The sea of uniformed pilots gave it a military feel which was certainly appropriate given, not only Jim Hartley's background, but that of so many of his fellow airmen. It was a solemn, heartbreaking event, and one that would never be forgotten by those in attendance.

When he was finally ready to be discharged from the hospital, Eastern Airlines offered to provide a special charter to bring my dad home. However, serially unwilling as he was to have a fuss made over him, and simply uncomfortable with the extra attention, he chose instead to be driven home by a friend. J.P. was scheduled for a trip on April 15, 1970, but the company gave him the day off so he could fly up to Boston and bring my father home. He had to rent the biggest station wagon he could find, and if he had to do it over again, probably would have rented a truck. In addition to himself and both of my parents, the haul included a large number of gifts, awards, and flower arrangements given to the captain of Flight 1320. When all was said and done Captain Wilbur received enough trophies, plaques, citations, medals, and frame-worthy letters of appreciation to more than fill a large room, let alone an oversized car.

Captain Wilbur continued his physical therapy and recuperation at home. The process was painful and tedious, but more than palatable given what could have been, and he rarely, if ever, complained. He hadn't seen Allison or I since the morning of March 17, and I'm told we greatly lifted his spirits. I can't imagine any man, even one as strong and emotionally reserved as my father, having the tools to make a quick and easy recovery from the violence he witnessed and was subjected to in the close confines of a DC-9 cockpit thousands of feet in the air. The pain associated with his injuries, and the fact that he was now grounded for the first time since his eighteen-month lay-off from Eastern in 1960/61, were constant reminders of that violence and loss.

On May 13, 1970, our family, and just about the entire Eastern Airlines family, were joined by dignitaries and high brass from throughout the airline industry on a trek to Miami, Florida, for a special ceremony. Eastern Airlines had recently erected a new training center on the grounds of Miami International Airport. The building would hence forth be known as the James E. Hartley Training Center. Eastern employees would eventually come to know it simply as, "The Hartley Building." Floyd D. Hall, then Eastern Airlines president and chairman of the board, delivered the dedication speech:

Thank you, Sam [Sam Higginbottom- Eastern Vice President who introduced him]. We of Eastern Airlines, as Mr. Higginbottom noted, look upon this new center as more than just a building. As a training center it is a living, yet symbolic representation of our continuing commitment to the Miami community, of which we consider ourselves an important part, and to the traveling public whom we serve. At the same time, we see it as a tribute to a man who personified the commitment and dedication to public service that is a way of life in our industry.

I used the word commitment and it is a word I chose carefully. A commitment is a pledge, and through the dedication of this building, we pledge several things. One is our reassertion of the importance of Miami to Eastern. As you all know, we recently acquired 125 acres of land adjacent to Doral Country Club. This training facility is the first of a number of expansions which we plan for Miami. Our commitment is also a pledge to maintain the highest levels of professional training possible, and finally is a continuing pledge to do all in our power to make flying as safe and as comfortable as possible for the traveling public. In our commercials we call it "making man as at home in the sky as he is on land."

In dedicating the training center, I think it's appropriate that we talk for a moment or two about the purpose of training in the airline industry. Ours is an industry of specializations. The vast majority of the people of Eastern are experts in their individual specializations. To achieve their expertise, they have undergone thorough training, and to enable them to remain up to date professionals, they must receive equally thorough and continuing training as new tools and techniques are added to their specializations. The end result of training is professionalism. A definition of professionalism, which I like, is that "it is a condition which results in the instinctive reaction always being the correct reaction." Certainly, this was the case with First Officer Hartley.

In thinking of training, most people think of the pilots whom we train here in the classrooms and simulators, and of the flight attendants who receive their initial and refresher training here. These are usually the only people passengers see, so they're the only ones they think of. The public rarely realizes that there are literally hundreds of people behind the scenes whose efforts are essential to the hour-by-hour operation of a passenger plane. But, in fact, for every Eastern Flight there are 130 people whose efforts make it all possible. We expect all of these people to achieve a high degree of professionalism and we spare no expense to provide them with the training that results in such professionalism.

Perhaps the highest tribute and praise which I can offer to James E. Hartley, in whose name we are dedicating this training center, is to say that he was a total professional. First Officer Hartley joined our company in 1966. A year later he was graduated from Eastern's pilot training program and was immediately assigned to John F. Kennedy Airport. In May 1967, he was transferred to Miami where he served as an instructor of second officers on the DC-8 training program. That in itself was unusual for a young man with our company little more than a year, and reflected the aptitude, ambition, and the excellence which he brought to his job.

However, James Hartley was at heart a flying officer and last year he requested a return to active line duty. He became a first officer based at John F. Kennedy International Airport in New York and, as we know, it was in the line of duty that he was killed as he was grappling with a gunman whose actions endangered the lives of 68 passengers and 5 crew members on an air-shuttle flight from Newark to Boston. First Officer Hartley's action, though it cost him his life, was instrumental in saving the lives of the passengers and his fellow crew members. First Officer Hartley and Captain Robert Wilbur, Jr., who safely landed the plane though he was wounded in both arms, displayed the courage, skill, professionalism, and the commitment that everyone has come to expect from pilots of Eastern Airlines and all carriers.

In a moment of crisis, First Officer Hartley acted instinctively, and his instinctive reaction was the correct one. We are proud to know that the thorough and extensive training which Captain Wilbur and First Officer Hartley received helped them to meet crisis and challenge. And I am certain that as future pilots, as well as mechanics, customer service agents, reservation agents, stewardesses, and other members of the people of Eastern receive their training here, they will be inspired by the example of Officer Hartley and will do their utmost to live up to the lofty ideal of public service which he typified.

You know the old saying about the world of politics, "Never let a crisis go to waste." I suppose that saying can also be applied to captains of industry. Mr. Floyd's speech was at once a tribute to the heroism of Jim Hartley and a public relations opportunity for Eastern Airlines. Never the less, the beautiful plaque which was unveiled that day adorned the front entrance to the James E. Hartley Training Center for the life of Eastern Airlines. It immortalized the man and the tragic event, and was, in and of itself, a moving tribute.

A few days after the dedication of the Hartley Building, my dad, now two months removed from the hijacking and with his injuries on the mend, took an extended and well-deserved vacation. Eastern was kind enough to finance the trip, and several international carriers provided first class tickets. He and my mother spent a week in Puerto Rico, followed by a month-long trip to Europe. They toured around London and the British Isles, flew to Denmark, and then on to Italy. They rented a car in Milan and drove all over Italy, Switzerland, and France before finally coming home. It was my mom's first time out of the country and it was certainly a trip she would never forget for many reasons. Seeing so many beautiful places she'd never seen before, especially for a girl from small town Scranton, Pennsylvania, was an amazing experience, and she got to do it with her husband whom she loves dearly. She also got to see my father smiling and enjoying himself for the first time since he came home from the hospital. He appeared, at least, to be coming back to life. For his part, my dad has always loved to travel, and the extended trip did much to lift his spirits. Touring around Europe brought back lots of happy memories from his air force days when he was stationed at Evreux-Fauville Air Force Base in France. When it was finally time to come home, however, he was chomping at the bit to get back to work.

Back in 1970, a diagnosis of post-traumatic stress disorder and the long-term psychological therapy which would have certainly accompanied it, wasn't nearly as in vogue as it is today. The idea of walking away from one's livelihood for a disability check, for reasons other than being physically unable to perform the job, was almost unheard of, and even if it were offered to my father, he would have laughed at the idea. He only knew how to do one thing and that was fly, and nothing but a dirt nap could derail his return. Nothing, that is, but the dreaded section-28 bid. Section-28 of the labor contract between the Airline Pilots' Association (ALPA) and management stated that senior pilots could bid down in order to change their domicile. In other words, an Eastern captain with more seniority than my father, who was flying a larger aircraft, and based out of Atlanta, for example, but wanted to move to the New York area, could put in a section-28 bid and bump him out of his captain's chair and back to the right seat. It's my understanding that circa 1970, for whatever reason, captains on the 727 were on the same pay scale as captains on the DC-9. The Boeing-727 was a significantly larger three-man crew aircraft with more range than the DC-9. This, of course, meant longer flights, more layovers, and more time spent away from home for the same money. Section-28 bids were usually offered on a semi-annual basis, and you couldn't bid down to a smaller aircraft unless you wanted to change location. New York–based pilots couldn't bump other New York–based pilots and Miami guys couldn't bump Miami guys, etc. The New York area was highly sought after at the time, and there were a good many senior pilots ready to take advantage of the section-28 bid. My dad was a very junior captain, only having received his stripes in December of 1969.

The pay cut and once again flying as a first officer would have made little difference to my dad as eager as he was to jump back on the horse and get back in the air. It made all the difference in the world, however, to upper level management at Eastern Airlines who had no intention of allowing their star captain to be demoted to first officer, no matter the circumstance. The company allowed him to return to work in late June 1970, but he was still grounded. Over his fervent objections, the company had him commuting daily to LaGuardia Airport where he joined a team that was working on a new navigation system called Decca. He retained his rank and continued to receive captain's pay. The Decca Navigation System never got off the ground, pardon the pun, and the undertaking was scrapped before long. Well before its demise, however, Captain Wilbur would get his wings back. In anticipation of captains' slots opening up, the company set him up with three weeks of recurrent simulator training in late July. The training was handled locally and allowed him to continue his physical therapy without any lengthy interruptions.

As a small child I remember that part of his therapy called for him to work with a material known as Theraplast, which looked a lot like silly putty. It consisted of slightly less than baseball-sized portions of putty-like material which came in various colors depending on its hardness and density. The therapy required him to repeatedly squeeze the Theraplast with his right hand in order to improve his grip strength, and as his forearm healed, and he grew stronger, he graduated to the next, harder/denser color. The different color Theraplast "putties" were in our home all throughout my childhood, and my sister and I would often play with them. We would sometimes ask our father to squeeze one as we'd simultaneously place one of our small fingers on the diamond shaped scar on the inside of his right forearm. It's difficult to describe, but the flesh within the diamond shaped border of the scar would cave in on itself, causing us to squeal with delight. At that point he would have almost certainly grabbed and tickled us, and this would usually be accompanied by a gentle toss into the air, followed by a smooth, sure-handed catch and release. Our dad was away so much when we were growing up, and those simple moments spent with him were always special.

His very first foray back into the captain's chair was flight 863, a DC-9 from LaGuardia to Miami on August 20, 1970. The trip itself was uneventful, but it conjured up feelings in my father that he could never fully explain. Somehow, something which was so familiar to him just didn't feel quite the same, and it was obviously more than just the five-month layoff. The last time he was in the air he had been victimized by a murderous gunman and suffered terrible injuries. He had witnessed the murder of his first officer and friend seated just three feet to his right and had had to continue fending off the crazed man while attempting to land his aircraft.

Sitting in the captain's chair for the very first time since the hijacking brought back his most vivid memories of the event. It certainly wasn't as if he didn't think about it at least fifty times a day, it was just that the familiarity of the setting had the unfortunate effect of sharpening his recall, and the powerful and horrific images running though his mind weren't easy to keep at bay.

11. Back in Boston

John Joseph Divivo, Jr., the man who was singularly responsible for the murder of First Officer James E. Hartley, Jr. and the attempted murder of Captain Robert M. Wilbur, Jr., as well as seventy others, was sitting in the Charles Street Jail in Boston awaiting his fate. But when would the powers that be end their squabbling and get on with it already? He had completed his observation period at Bridgewater State Psychiatric Hospital and was deemed fit to stand trial. But who would drop the axe on Divivo and grab the headlines for such a high-profile case? The battle between the FBI and local Massachusetts authorities remained heated throughout the summer of 1970. The Feds, however, had already flexed some serious muscle in this jurisdictional pissing contest that would, very likely, have tipped the scales in their favor had a prosecution of Divivo ultimately become necessary. In concert with the Department of Transportation and the FAA, Federal Investigators confiscated Flight 1320's cabin voice recorder, flight data recorder, and the air traffic control recording of their transmissions with Captain Wilbur and First Officer Hartley.

The following excerpt from internal FBI memos make it clear that they had serious concerns as to the state's competence in pursuing the investigation. "Efforts are being made to locate and interview passengers from the passenger list obtained from Eastern Airlines, which is not very detailed in as much as it was a shuttle flight. This is necessary because State Police released more than half of the passengers who were aboard the aircraft after it landed at Logan Airport before they were ever interviewed by anyone, and they did not even ascertain their identities."

In addition, FBI correspondence alluded to an on-going hostility toward the FBI by the Massachusetts State Police dating back many years. Special Agent J.J. Casten, in a memo to Assistant FBI Director John Mohen, regarding this open hostility between the two agencies wrote: "…this organization is a poorly run, poorly administered police agency, and personnel assignments appear to be based purely on political considerations; further, Lieutenant O'Holloran, according to information furnished by our Boston Office, still leaks information to the criminal element. For that reason, our relations with this agency have continued on a circumspect basis and we have afforded it no training or National Academy assistance." In a rather long diatribe, Special Agent Casten described the jealousy that many high-ranking Massachusetts State Police Officers had for the FBI. This jealousy, according to Mr. Casten, stemmed from disparities in salary, prestige, and respect.

In 1964 the FBI initiated restrictions on the Massachusetts State Police from participation in its National Academy Training Programs. These training programs are held at the FBI's training headquarter in Quantico, Virginia, four times a year. Candidates for the ten-week training program are selected from a nationwide pool of locally nominated law enforcement personnel. Military Police and select international nominees are also eligible. Among many other criteria, candidates must be in excellent physical condition, must have an excellent character, and enjoy a reputation for professional integrity. According to the FBI, candidates must have an interest in law enforcement as a public service, possess qualities of leadership, and enjoy the confidence and respect of fellow officers. Although the FBI needs to select law enforcement officers who can physically handle a rigorous ten-week training program, the agency was, and is, even more concerned with the character of those participating in its trainings. There are times when sensitive information is disseminated during the course of training. Such information could potentially be used to undermine, or worse, endanger law enforcement. There is always the possibility that confidential information could be leaked by unscrupulous individuals for personal gain. In learning of the lack of cooperation with Federal Authorities by the Massachusetts State Police in the investigation of the hijacking of Eastern Airlines Flight 1320, FBI Director J. Edgar Hoover sent out a terse directive to his training academy shot callers which said simply, "See that no candidate for National Academy from Massachusetts State Police are solicited." Although this directive was, for all intents and purposes, already standard operating procedure when it came to the FBI's dealings with the Massachusetts State Police, the fact that it was verbalized by the director was an embarrassment to Massachusetts law enforcement, particularly in the Boston area.

The acrimony which clearly existed between the Massachusetts State Police and the Federal Bureau of Investigation, and all the infighting and jurisdictional squabbling that took place following the hijacking of Eastern Airlines Flight 1320, and whatever negative impact that may or may not have had on a prosecution of the hijacker would ultimately become a non-issue. On October 31, 1970, while incarcerated in the Charles Street Jail awaiting trial for his crimes, John Joseph Divivo, Jr. finally succeeded in taking his own life where twice before he had failed so dramatically. Jail officials determined that he hanged himself in his cell using a scarf. His body was discovered at approximately 3:02 a.m. Maybe for Divivo the third time was the charm, or maybe fate finally decided to grant him his wish, or maybe, just maybe, the powers that be decided to be merciful to everyone involved, and simply looked the other way. Interesting that a man who had just recently, and so publicly, tried to kill himself, along with so many others, and who had a previous documented suicide attempt, was allowed to be in possession of an article which could so easily be used for that very purpose. Authorities clearly knew that Divivo was suicidal, yet it appears that, at a minimum, no extraordinary measures were taken to prevent him from reaching his ultimate goal. Either way the boogie man was dead, and on Halloween no less.

12. The Reluctant Hero

It turned out that my father's time on the DC-9 would soon come to an end. On November 1, 1970, Captain Wilbur began four and a half weeks of recurrent training and ground school for the Boeing 727. This time the training would take place in Miami, Florida, at the newly minted James E. Hartley Training Center.

Returning so soon to the building which now bore the name of his fallen first officer could not have been easy for my father, although he said that the building itself didn't conjure up new feelings within him, or exacerbate those he already felt. He describes his feelings as a combination of pride and sadness. Pride in the bravery and heroism and sacrifice made by Jim, and sadness in his passing. To put into proper perspective his own cursory self-analysis, and the lack of depth in his description of his feelings, one has to understand that my father isn't a man prone to strong emotion. Even more, he wouldn't be willing to share that emotion with anyone, not even those closest to him.

For more than a year following the hijacking, awards and accolades poured in from everywhere. In addition to phoning my father in the hospital, President Richard Nixon sent him a congratulatory letter on March 19, 1970, which read:

"The bravery and cool headedness you demonstrated during your recent dramatic flight to Logan International Airport have won the admiration of all of your fellow citizens. I am sure your recovery will be hastened by the satisfaction of knowing that your valor has saved so many lives and I want to send my own congratulations and best wishes to you."

On March 19 the New Jersey General Assembly passed a resolution commending Jim and my dad for their bravery and heroism. County and city governments in New Jersey, Massachusetts, Florida, and Texas followed suit, as did the United States Senate, which honored Captain Wilbur and First Officer Hartley on March 24, 1970, with Senate Resolution #375. In June my dad was named one of Bergen County New Jersey's Ten Greatest Men, and in August of 1970, he was awarded the Silver Cross by the United States Legion of Valor.

The Daedalian Civilian Air Safety Award is presented annually to the captain and crew of a civilian airliner which demonstrated the most outstanding judgement and/or heroism above and beyond normal operational requirements. Not surprisingly, Captain Wilbur and First Officer Hartley won the award in 1970. My dad donated the large Daedalian trophy to Eastern Airlines where it adorned the entranceway to the James E. Hartley Training Center in Miami, Florida. It was placed right under the Hartley dedication plaque, just where my father thought it should be. With the dissolution of Eastern Airlines in 1991, the trophy inexplicably disappeared, and its whereabouts are still a mystery to this day.

In late March of 1971, a little more than a year after the hijacking, our family moved from our small cape cod in Fair Lawn to a nice four-bedroom center hall colonial on a quiet dead-end street in Fairfield, New Jersey. Over the next several years, my mom took it upon herself to unbox and unwrap most of my father's awards and citations, which, I'm told, had been glaringly conspicuous in their absence. They were ultimately displayed on the walls and on shelves in the most lived in and comfortable room in our home. Every house has one. Call it a den, living room, TV room, rec room; we called ours, "The family room." My father didn't kick up too big a fuss about the display. I think he knew he'd be fighting an uphill battle that he just wouldn't win.

I remember walking around the room with my sister, Allison, just marveling at it all. We'd ask a million questions about the awards and letters and, of course, about the hijacking. We got our best information from Mom, who didn't mind in the least talking about our father, the hero. I memorized every award and framed piece of correspondence on the walls and shelves of our family room, what each one said, and whom it was from.

Our father was away on trips a lot when we were growing up, but when he was home, he'd spend time with us in the family room, watching TV, or playing board games, or whatever else we might be doing. Looking back at it now, I don't recall ever seeing him stand directly in front of his awards looking at them. In fact, it always seemed to me that his gaze was almost purposeful in its avoidance of that area of the room. It didn't strike any of us as terribly strange, but it was something we noticed. When we had a question, or one of our friends had a question, or a family friend or relative had a question, he'd politely answer it, but without expounding on it, even a little bit. The vibe he gave off was pretty clear, and, over time, the questions eventually stopped. I suspect that he never felt completely comfortable in that room.

A number of years later, he and his friend Walter finished our basement. Complete with a pool table, comfortable couches, and a nice TV, it was a real man cave. Devoid of any memorabilia from the hijacking, it served as a useful respite for my father over the years. With no visible reminders of that traumatic event it became, I believe, his fortress of solitude.

Every award, every citation, every accolade he would ultimately receive following Eastern Airlines Flight 1320 (and there were a great many), brought back all the painful memories in a public way. Even more, they highlighted the obvious fact that, against all odds, he'd survived the ordeal, and the man seated just three feet to his right did not. Although he was certainly thankful beyond words to be alive and reunited with his wife and children, with his survival came unexplained feelings of guilt, and those feelings would never completely disappear. Below is just a sampling of many of the awards and accolades he received following the hijacking

Order of Daedalians

DAEDALIAN CIVILIAN AIR SAFETY AWARD
1970
Captain Robert M. Wilbur, Jr.
First Officer James E. Hartley, Jr., (Posthumously)
Eastern Air Lines

On 17 March 1970, the pilot of an Eastern Air Lines DC-9, Captain Robert M. Wilbur, Jr., and his co-pilot, James E. Hartley, Jr., displayed extra-ordinary heroism, courage and professional competence in averting a major air disaster and saving the lives of the passengers and crew.

The occurrence took place in the Boston terminal area during an approach for a landing at Logan International Airport when a passenger produced a gun and demanded to see the captain. After entering the cockpit, he ordered that the aircraft be flown to the east and that the captain advise him when two minutes of fuel remained. The flight then proceeded east until approximately 20 miles east of the Boston VORTAC when Captain Wilbur informed the gunman that he was low on fuel and asked if he could start back inbound. The assailant agreed. During the trip inbound, the assailant shot and wounded both the captain and the first officer. Although mortally wounded, First Officer Hartley disarmed the assailant and shot him twice. Captain Wilbur took the weapon as the gunman fell to the floor and First Officer Hartley slumped over in his seat and died as a result of a wound that penetrated the chest area. Captain Wilbur was shot in the right forearm and left bicep.

The captain increased the speed of the aircraft to 250 knots and informed the Boston Approach Control that his co-pilot had been shot and that a doctor, ambulance and police would be needed upon arrival. Despite being wounded himself, with his co-pilot slumped in the seat and the assailant lying on the floor by the jumpseat, Captain Wilbur successfully performed the complex task of returning the plane and passengers to a safe landing at Logan International Airport.

The heroism of First Officer Hartley in sacrificing his own life to preserve the safety of others and the superb airmanship of Captain Wilbur in bringing the aircraft to a safe landing under conditions of maximum adversity, reflect the highest ideals and objectives of the Daedalian Civilian Air Safety Award.

The Daedalian Civilian Air Safety Award Trophy which my father donated to the James E. Hartley Training Center in Miami. The Previous page is the dedication letter written by the Order of the Daedalian bestowing the award on Captain Wilbur and First Officer Hartley posthumously

Legion of Valor Silver Cross with accompanying citation

Various medals from the FAA, the Airline Pilots Association and the United Nations. My dad can't quite recall the circumstance, but he received a pretty cool autographed picture from George H. W. Bush. Then just a lowly freshman congressman from Texas

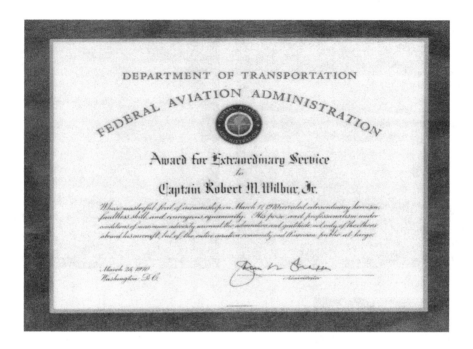

FAA Award for Outstanding Heroism and
Citation from the Florida Department of Commerce

To: Captain Robert H. Wilbur, Jr.

In a moment of extreme crisis, the sense of moral responsibility, professional ability and all of the physical and mental resources a man acquires and develops up to that point in his life are revealed and tested to their utmost. Many fail these tests--few succeed.

On the night of March 17, 1970, while in command of an Eastern Air Lines DC-9 approaching Boston, you were put to such a test and avoided a major disaster in a manner that can only be described as exceeding the generally accepted limits of human endurance and accomplishment.

In spite of severe mental anguish and stress, extensive personal physical injury and the lack of assistance from your co-pilot who had been mortally wounded, you demonstrated an extraordinary degree of pilot skill and concern for your 76 passengers and crew by landing your aircraft safely and without incident at Logan International Airport.

Your outstanding performance under these extremely adverse and almost unbelievable conditions are irrefutable evidence to your eminent professional competence and selfless concern for your fellow man.

We, the members of the Massachusetts Port Authority, on behalf of the people of the Commonwealth of Massachusetts, commend you for your exemplary and heroic act.

Citation form the Massachusetts Port Authority

United States Senate Resolution 375

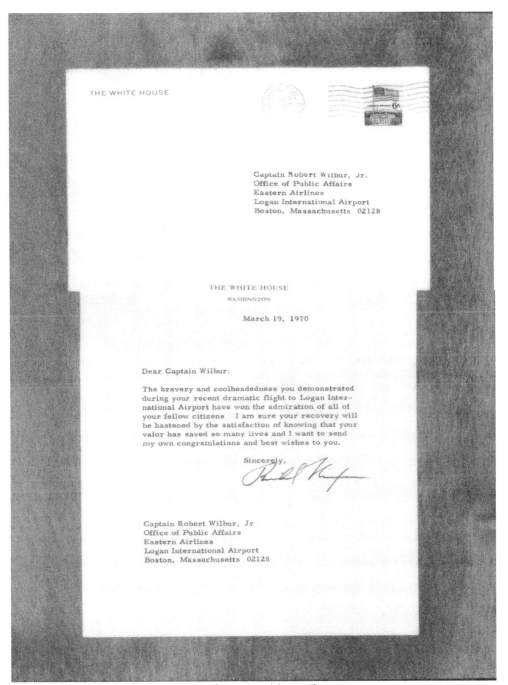

Letter from President Nixon

13. Life Goes On

Life, of course, continued for the surviving passengers and crew of Flight 1320. The experience affected each of them differently and, over the years, their lives would take some interesting and, sometimes, surprising paths.

Being in such close proximity to gunfire and death had a major impact on flight attendant Christine Peterson. After the incident, she took advantage of her much needed leave of absence. Her friend Marjorie said she returned home to Buffalo and the two, "…went on a month-long drinking binge together, we had a great time just talking and spending time together, but Christine eventually wanted to get back to work."

Unfortunately for Christine, her dream of a long career as a flight attendant was over. Gone was the feeling of joy and freedom she had previously associated with flying. Upon her return to active duty, being in the air gave her an uneasy, uncomfortable feeling, which quickly turned into out and out fear. Passengers were all seen as potentially dangerous to her, and each trip brought with it the mental anguish of remembering the image of a lifeless Jim Hartley being carried from Flight 1320.

Christine wasn't of a mind to settle back in Buffalo. She turned in her wings and got a job in reservations in Atlanta, Georgia, but it just wasn't the same. Christine left Eastern Airlines in 1971 and went to work in the office of a local doctor near her home in Jonesboro, Georgia.

The disappointment she felt over a career cut short gradually faded over time, and Christine eventually began to heal. Although she didn't love it, Christine liked her new job, and she really liked her new boss. The two developed a close relationship and began dating. It was the happiest she'd been in quite a long time, and a wedding was eventually planned in Christine's hometown of Buffalo, New York. Following the nuptials, she and the doctor planned to return to the Atlanta area to begin their new lives together. I'm sure we've all seen romantic comedies and TV sitcoms where one of the characters is left at the altar, but it can't be terribly funny in real life. The doctor called Christine thirty minutes before the ceremony was to start and said his daughter was sick, and that he couldn't make the trip to Buffalo. She never saw or spoke to him again.

Christine licked her wounds, made one final trip to Georgia to clear out her apartment, and moved back home to Buffalo, immersing herself in the warmth of family and friends. Then she did what girls from Buffalo do, what graduates from Bryant & Stratton do, she got an office job. First with a printing company called Graphic Controls, and then as a clerk for a local food service distributor. In 1975 she married Richard Kirwan, a police officer working in nearby Kenmore, New York. They had two children, Michael and Sean, before eventually separating in 1980. Another marriage and divorce would follow, and more jobs would come and go. Christine was somewhat restless in her sleepy home town, but then I suppose she always knew she would be. According to her best friend, Margie, she was happy with her life, happy to watch her sons grow into fine young men, and happy with the safety and security that a close-knit family and community provide.

Following the tragedy of September 11, 2001, NBC's *Dateline* interviewed my father at his home in Palm Beach Gardens, Florida. Seeing him after so many years brought back a flood of memories, both pleasant and painful. Christine felt compelled to reach out and was able to find him through various Eastern Airlines contacts. She placed a call to my parent's home in late September 2001. To the best of their recollections neither of them remember ever having spoken to the other at any point after the incident more than thirty-one years prior. Christine told my dad that she was glad to hear he was alive and well, and that he and my mom were together and happy after all these years. Christine told him that she quit flying after the hijacking and moved back home to Buffalo. She thanked him for somehow finding a way to bring their plane down safely that night. She told him that she had two beautiful children, and that her life in upstate New York was quiet and routine, but that she was very happy. I'm sure that some part of her wondered how her life might have turned out if the traumatic events of March 17, 1970, never happened.

On February 21, 2004, Christine Peterson Kirwan passed away after a long battle with a rare disease called Amyloidosis. Family and friends were never far away during her two-year struggle with the illness, and were, of course, at her bedside to comfort her at the end.

***

Arlene Albino said that, without a doubt, the traumatic nature of the event altered the course of her life. She had been dating a nice young Italian boy named Abelardo Espinosa. The two had met just three months earlier at the Crow's Nest in Hasbrouck Heights and, after hearing about the hijacking, Abelardo raced up to Boston to see his girlfriend. Arlene described how they emphatically declared their love for each other, after which, she asked him to marry her. Arlene would eventually come to realize that the two weren't very compatible, but that her near-death experience, the very real thought that she would die without ever having a family of her own, caused her to rush into marriage prematurely. She and Abelardo split up after seven and a half years together. This time frame roughly coincides with Arlene's departure from the airline industry.

Arlene went on to say that, "For years I carried around a lot of baggage." The incident left her with feelings of intense anxiety, depression, and paranoia, feelings that, today, would be described as PTSD. Still, Arlene says, "I loved my job, and part of me wasn't ready to leave it. It's like being in a bad marriage. There were so many things I still loved about the job, and so many things, especially after the incident, that made me hate it." While gradually working on her exit strategy, Arlene gritted her teeth and continued to fly. Living at home with her parents and earning a steady paycheck afforded her the opportunity to go back to school part-time. She attended classes at Montclair State College majoring in psychology.

On June 5, 1975, Arlene worked her very last flight, a trip from Newark to San Juan, Puerto Rico, and back. The weather was bad, the flight was rough, and the passengers were particularly short tempered. Arlene could no longer ignore, or repress, the feelings that such a flight produced in her. She would go out on a six-month paid stress leave, but never return. Unemployment, waitressing, and even a job as a Bergen County probation officer would follow. This was all in conjunction with Arlene's drive to continue her education. She finally earned her bachelor's degree in psychology in 1978, and started law school at Seton Hall University that same fall.

Arlene felt more comfortable and at ease in the academic environment of law school. This, coupled with the passing of time, allowed a gradual healing process and made her optimistic about the future. It was at law school that Arlene met fellow student, Richard Ralph. The two hit it off immediately and were married on November 21, 1981. They are both successful lawyers today and continue to be happily married with two beautiful daughters. With the trauma of the hijacking of Eastern Airlines Flight 1320 drifting further and further in her rearview mirror, Arlene is able to look at it from a healthier perspective. She realizes just how lucky she was to survive the ordeal. She acknowledges the sheer magnitude of the event, understanding that the hijacking is a significant part of aviation history. She lauds the sheer will and the unbelievable sacrifice made by her first officer, Jim Hartley, that night and is thankful beyond words for the skill and bravery displayed by Captain Wilbur.

***

When I asked Sandy Saltzer if the hijacking, particularly the tragic death of First Officer Jim Hartley, and the trauma of her own near-death experience, moved her to make any life altering decisions, she paused for only a moment before answering, "No." "My father taught me that when you fall off a horse you have to get right back on." Sandy continued to fly and enjoyed a twenty-year career as a flight attendant, retiring with the collapse of Eastern Airlines in 1989. She went on to say that both of her parents lived through the Great Depression, and she witnessed their unflappable resolve whenever times were tough growing up. "It was a terrific lesson for me, I learned independence and self-confidence, and I was never the type to get too rattled."

Born and raised in the Rochester area of New York, Sandy was the eldest of four children by a pretty wide margin. She would have the luxury of being a kid, with the unfettered freedom to pursue her own interests above all others, until the ripe old age of 10. Sandy had two hard working blue collar parents, and when siblings; Mark, Caroline and Anne Marie came along, she was thrust into the role of caregiver. Over time, she became so comfortable and at ease in this role, and the required skills became so entrenched in her, that, for Sandy, it would eventually become a life's pursuit.

Sandy was married from 1980 to 1985. Following her divorce, she decided to go back to school part-time for her master's degree in counseling, which today would roughly be the equivalent of a master's in social work. She was living in Atlanta, Georgia, at the time and completed the requirements for her degree in 1989 from Georgia State. The caregiver in Sandy, it appears, could no longer be contained. What would have happened if Eastern Airlines didn't file for Chapter-7 Liquidation? The company officially ceased operations on January 18, 1991, although for all intents and purposes it died in 1989. Sandy wouldn't speculate as to whether she would have left without the push. That being said, with her education complete, and her career as a flight attendant over, Sandy returned to upstate New York, where she would work as an oncology nurse at Clifton Springs Hospital, in Clifton Springs, New York, for the next twenty-one years.

In 1993, Sandy, along with nursing colleagues, Jean Cass and Judy Nadal, established a two-bed hospice for terminally ill cancer patients in Clifton Springs called The House of John. In the years since, six additional houses have been established all over upstate New York, each one modeled after The House of John, and each servicing anywhere from eighty to a hundred and twenty patients a year. The houses are staffed solely by volunteers and are funded through direct donations and annual fundraisers. Sandy retired from nursing in 2010, at the age of sixty-six. Her mother, Margaret, who had been diagnosed with dementia some years earlier, had begun to deteriorate and was in need of full-time care. With the hospices up and running smoothly, and with a second long career behind her, who better to take on the job than her daughter, the caregiver.
Over the years, her impact on the lives of thousands of people afflicted with cancer cannot possibly be quantified or overstated. I wonder if any of Sandy's patients were

aware that none of it would have been possible without the extraordinary heroism of two men.

Flight attendants Christine Peterson, Sandy Saltzer, and Arlene Albino each received the Distinguished Cabin Service Award for their efforts on board Eastern Airlines Flight 1320.

***

Stephen Fowler, the Eastern Airlines chauffeur who drove my mother to Mass General that fateful day, went on to have a lengthy career with Eastern, separating from the company after their bankruptcy in 1989. He worked in the insurance business for about ten years or so, and finished up his working career as a customs/immigration inspector in Calexico, California, on the Mexican border.

***

Passenger Manny Abrams had flown the shuttle a number of times before March 17, 1970. He certainly had no reason to suspect that anything out of the ordinary would happen on that trip. He remembers thinking that the 7:30 p.m. flight might just get him home on time to kiss thirteen-year-old Zoe and ten-year-old Katy goodnight. He said that, at the time, his consulting business was taking him away from home too often and costing him more and more precious time with his family. Manny closed the business shortly after his experience on Flight 1320, deciding to work closer to home.

Today, Manny is a ninety-three-year-old retiree still living in Natick, Massachusetts. He lost Barbara, his beautiful wife of more than fifty years, on December 20, 2009.

Daughters Zoe and Katy are now sixty-one and fifty-eight respectively, and both have families of their own. Manny is an accomplished violinist and avid reader. He still plays in a local orchestra and meets with members of his book club whenever he can. He often thinks about that long-ago St. Patrick's Day flight home. The memories remain far greener than any ninety-three-year-old man should expect from an event that took place some forty-nine years ago and counting. The once-in-a-lifetime, almost surreal nature of the experience, along with its associated trauma, only account for part of the reason Manny recalls the event with such clarity. The rest can be attributed to a unique relationship he maintains with fellow Flight 1320 survivor, Peggy McLoughlin.

***

Peggy McLoughlin was briefly interviewed by the FBI days after the incident and simply went back to her life as a student. According to Peggy, "It was an unbelievable situation that I luckily emerged from, and since there was so little made out of it in the media, I guess I picked up on that same mood. The lack of attention almost made it seem like it never happened, so I just moved on from it."

Peggy earned her degree in elementary education and theology from Boston College in 1973. She was a full-time high school teacher while continuing her education, eventually earning a master's degree in library science from Simmons College. Peggy also found time for marriage and family. Today, her four children, Luke, Ryan, Clare, and William, range in age from thirty-one to thirty-nine and are highly successful in their own right. Peggy has two beautiful grandchildren, Daniel and Jane, and she sees her family quite often relishing every moment.

Peggy most certainly shared her story of the hijacking with friends and family over the years, characterizing the event as a unique and interesting anecdote, but little more. She admits that her youth and immaturity at the time of the hijacking colored her perspective of the event, causing her to miss its greater significance. For thirty-nine years she never spoke to another passenger, or crew member, about the hijacking. Then came the "Miracle on the Hudson."

On January 15, 2009, US Airways Flight 1549, an A320 Airbus, took off from New York's LaGuardia Airport bound for Charlotte, North Carolina. Just after takeoff, the aircraft lost both engines and was forced to make an emergency water landing on the Hudson River. The NTSB investigation revealed that multiple bird strikes to both engines had caused their failure. The media frenzy was immediate and seemingly never ending, and the aircraft's captain, Chesley "Sully" Sullenberger, was hailed a hero.

This got Peggy thinking about her own experience, and she seemed to have a long overdue epiphany, realizing the magnitude of what took place aboard Eastern Airlines Flight 1320. Nearly thirty-seven years after the event, Peggy McLoughlin was now determined to find and thank the man who played such a key role in saving her life. Below is the letter she wrote to my father on March 9, 2009. Within the envelope she enclosed a picture of her family.

60 Clyde Street
Newton, Massachusetts
March 9, 2009

Dear Captain Wilbur,

Captain JP Trestani learned of my interest in locating you through the Retired Eastern Airlines Pilots Association and forwarded me your address.

I was a passenger on your flight that was hijacked on March 17, 1970. I was a 19-year-old college student returning from my home in Livingston, NJ to Boston College.

The recent "Miracle on the Hudson"

brought the whole experience back to me so vividly. I realized I had never thanked you for what you and Captain Hartley did for me and so many others that day. I was so young and so stunned (I merely got on the trolley without speaking to anyone and went back to the dorm) that I almost could not believe what I had experienced. I hope you will accept my grateful thanks for the most amazing rescue of us on that day.

I was sitting on the left side of the plane as it faced the cockpit and was quite aware of everything that was going on.

- 3 -

I saw the hijacker go into the cockpit and turn almost smiling as though he had been pushed up to the front.

I watched the stewardess close the door and later the sounds of shouts on the and the bullets.

It is all as vivid to me as though it were yesterday — and now it is 39 years later. You probably hardly need me to recount all of what I saw as you lived it and saved us.

What strikes me now - these many years later - is how young you and Captain Hartley and the crew were! And how skillful!

When I think of Captain Sullenberger landing in the Hudson, he was 57 with a full and long career behind him to do it. You were so much younger.

- 4 -

Speaking of Captain Sullenberger - a friend of mine recently met him and related the story of your dramatic save of our flight. He was riveted to the story and asked him to repeat it twice. He said he was in college at the time.

I have enclosed a picture of my family. I'm on the far right - and a far way from being that girl on the flight! My oldest son is 31 - almost your age when you flew that day. I've had a very happy and full life. Thank you for it.

I will always be grateful to you and Captain Hartley.

With utmost appreciation and thanks.

Peggy Coyle McLoughlin

In her efforts to locate the retired Eastern Airlines captain, Peggy enlisted the help of a local reporter named Adrian Walker who wrote for the *Boston Globe*. She told Adrian her story and he offered to help her locate my father. Adrian wound up writing a small piece about the hijacking and about Peggy's desire to thank my father. The article appeared in the paper on March 20, 2009. Manny Abrams just happened to run across that newspaper article, which prompted him to talk about his own experiences with some of the guys in his book club. It turns out that one of the guys had a sister who was friends with Peggy, and Manny wasted little time reaching out to her. The two have shared a unique friendship ever since. They live only minutes from each other, and unbeknownst to either of them, Peggy had been teaching a yoga class for years in an adjoining room to where Manny's orchestra rehearsed.

Today, Peggy is a librarian at Wellesley Free Library in Wellesley, Massachusetts, and at the age of sixty-nine, she still teaches yoga classes in the chapel at the First Baptist Church of Newton. Manny's orchestra still rehearses in the main church, and the two routinely see each other. Manny and Peggy try to make it a point to call each other every St. Patrick's Day. In addition to catching up on their day-to-day lives, the two survivors of Eastern Airlines Flight 1320 still talk about how lucky they feel to be alive, and how grateful they are for the incredible bravery and skill displayed by the two men in the line of fire that night.

***

Captain Wilbur would returned to the skies in earnest, flying the Boeing 727 for the next thirteen years. These were good years, not only for his career, but for family as well. The only therapy available to him was in the cockpit, and with each successful takeoff and landing, and in concert with the slow and steady healing process that comes with the passage of time, he moved beyond the terrible memories of Flight 1320 and the nightmares that followed. In 1983 he moved on to the A-300 Airbus, followed by the Lockheed L/1011. He stayed busy and was all too often absent from our home. When I think about today's world, and the thought that my father would almost certainly be forced to sit down with a psychiatrist and open up about his feelings in order to get his wings back, it makes me laugh. It might have caused him to quit. For my father, flying was the best therapy, and I think, eventually, he was able to find the joy in it again. He was, after all, at his very core, a pilot.

14. Like Father Like Son?

As I've said before, we as a family almost never spoke of the hijacking. As my sister and I grew older we might have possessed the maturity to understand the gravity of what took place, but without any real dialogue on the subject, it almost became this mythical thing, too far removed, too unreal to grasp.

I was fifteen years old the one and only time I was on an airplane with my father at the controls. It was the night of August 8, 1983, aboard Flight 917 from Newark to San Juan, Puerto Rico. The return trip on the morning of August 10 gave us about twenty-eight hours, just enough time for a brief father/son hangout. My dad flew an additional round-trip leg in between, leaving me at the crew hotel with strict instructions to stay put. This was at the very tail end of his time aboard the Boeing 727, a plane which he'd been flying for roughly thirteen years. My mom, who would shortly be diagnosed with Crohn's disease, was suffering through another drawn-out battle with her stomach. She suggested the trip, at least in part to carve out some alone time for herself during a pretty rough stretch.

In 1983, regulations regarding passenger access to the cockpit on commercial aircraft were worlds apart from what they are today, and I got to ride the jump seat right behind my dad, the captain. Having the opportunity to watch him work up close, to see him fly, was a thrill I'll never forget. The three-man crew carried out their duties in a smooth, sure handed synchronicity that was impressive to watch. This was a night flight, and the seemingly endless array of brightly lit instruments in the cockpit looked to me like stars on a crystal-clear night, and they spoke to the expertise necessary to operate such an aircraft. First Officer Ellis Moore and Second Officer Charlie Paar couldn't have been nicer or more accommodating to me during the three-hour flight.

Sitting in the dark 727 cockpit, illuminated only by the ambient light of the glowing instruments, and experiencing first-hand the close quarters under which pilots have to work, I couldn't help but think about Flight 1320, and how truly horrifying it must have been. What on earth would possess a man to ever climb back in? I hadn't thought about the hijacking in a long time and my presence in that cockpit with my dad brought to the surface many of the old questions. Yet knowing all too well how uncomfortable the topic was to my father, I just let it go. He flew the first leg of the trip and, just as I'd always imagined it in my mind, he landed his plane with an unrivaled precision. I'd been on many planes before and, of course, since that flight, but I can't recall a smoother landing. If a full cup of coffee had been on the dashboard not a drop would have spilled. It was as if his aircraft were a butterfly with sore feet. It was easy to see, even at my tender young age, that he enjoyed his work and, when I commented on the overall flight, particularly the landing, he seemed to get a real kick out of my reaction.

Six years later, just a couple of months into Eastern Airlines' Strike, I graduated from college. I was a business major and, to the very best of my recollection, had never expressed any real interest in flying. I'm not sure what motivated me to pursue a pilot's license, but pursue it I did, even after an awful introductory flight out of Essex County Airport in Fairfield. Rough weather and a surly flight instructor who wanted to be anywhere else but flying single engine Cessnas with beginner pilots, nearly made me lose my lunch. Still I pressed on, researching low cost flight schools and working my ass off throughout that summer to save the necessary funds. An exhaustive search led me to Mustang Aviation in Jonesboro, Arkansas. The owner confirmed that I could obtain my license in as little as six weeks and at a cost of roughly $3,500, including housing.

In early October, 1989, I hopped on a one-way flight to Memphis, Tennessee and made my way to Jonesboro Municipal Airport some 65 miles away. On November 20th, less than six weeks later, I passed my check-ride and became a certified private pilot. I was quite proud of the accomplishment and couldn't wait to show my dad. He wasn't in the best of moods during that time, given what was happening with Eastern, but he demonstrated a modicum of enthusiasm when I showed him my freshly minted license. Still, it took nearly four years for us to take our one and only flight together with me at the controls, but the experience was priceless. It was October 1, 1993, during one of his brief visits home from the other side of the world.

He didn't say a whole lot during the flight, he just looked out the window and occasionally glanced in my direction, and I remember being more than a little nervous. We were doing touch and go's at Essex County Airport and on one of the downwind legs he turned to me and said, "Robbie, I think you're a little bit low son," to which I replied in as snarky a tone as I could muster, "You're not PIC (Pilot in Command) on this flight pop, I am." He ignored the jab and just said something like, "Okay that's fine," and continued scanning the horizon. It had to be less than thirty seconds later that the controller comes over the radio with, "Cessna N68485, the traffic pattern altitude is 1100 feet, were showing you at 850." We just looked at each other and cracked up. He probably hadn't been in a small 2-seater like that since his early air force training days in 1955, but he had more flying instincts in his pinkie than I had in my whole body, and then some.

My final flight was on June 30, 2000. I just couldn't drag myself up there for the three take-offs and landings I had to have every ninety days to keep my flight status current. I never fell in love with it, not anywhere near like he did. Pointing an analytic finger in my own direction, it's pretty easy to understand why I worked so hard to become a pilot, an activity for which I had no particular interest or aptitude, and one fraught with such genuine peril for all but those individuals who are steadfastly committed to the vocation. I could tell you story after story of half-assed preparation and overall reckless disregard for basic safety standards that could easily have ended in tragedy for myself and my all too trusting passengers. But flying was what my father did, it was what he was, and just by doing it, by being one of them, even on the very smallest of scales, and being able to talk with him about it, made me feel somehow closer to him.

15. The End Of An Era

Throughout the 1960s and 70s, Eastern Airlines and its employees had experienced a great many years of labor peace. However, in the early to mid-1980s, in the wake of deregulation, Eastern, like many other established carriers, began to feel the squeeze of increased competition. Although profitable in 1985, the company had lost money in each of the previous five years, and by 1986 was heavily in debt. Enter Columbia University and Harvard Business School graduate Francisco Anthony Lorenzo, whose first major foray into the world of commercial aviation came in 1972 when, at just thirty-two years of age, he acquired struggling Texas International Airlines. Lorenzo quickly gained a reputation as a union buster, slashing costs at the airline by forcing huge wage and benefit cuts to its employees. By filing for bankruptcy, he was able to void union contracts, which allowed him virtual cart blanch to pay his, now non-union employees, a small percentage of their previous wage, and by doing so, he reaped huge profits.

His experience with Texas International only seemed to whet his appetite for more acquisition. In 1980, Lorenzo created a holding company called Texas Air Corporation, under which he would eventually acquire numerous major airlines, including: Continental, New York Air, Eastern, Peoples Express, and Frontier, along with several regional carriers. In 1985 he attempted a takeover of troubled TWA but lost out to fellow corporate raider, Carl Icahn.

In the wee hours of the morning on February 24, 1986, at approximately 3:15 a.m., following a lengthy and contentious meeting, Eastern's board of directors, including chairman of the board and former NASA astronaut, Frank Borman, voted 15–4 in favor of selling their airline to Frank Lorenzo and Texas Air Corporation. They sold out for somewhere in the neighborhood of six hundred million dollars. And at that point, I'm fairly certain, Eddie Rickenbacker, former head of Eastern Airlines in its early hay day, and World War I flying ace, officially turned over in his grave. This once proud company which had been in existence since 1926 would quickly, and unceremoniously, be carved up. Over the next several years Lorenzo would follow the same playbook which had served him so well in the past with both Texas International and Continental Airlines. When existing union contracts at Eastern expired, draconian cuts to salary and benefits were demanded.

In March of 1989, Eastern Airlines' largest union, the International Association of Machinists (IAM), in the face of such proposed cuts to their wages and benefits, went on strike. The pilots, knowing that their heads would be on the chopping block next, walked out in solidarity. Predictably, Mr. Lorenzo filed for bankruptcy. The final outcome, however, would be different than it was with both Texas International and Continental Airlines. Rather than seeking to void established union contracts in an effort to cut labor costs and wash away the large debt load at Eastern, both of which would be achieved through a successful bankruptcy, Mr. Lorenzo took it a step further, and he did so with the full knowledge and blessing of the United States Bankruptcy Courts. A controversial ruling during the bankruptcy proceeding went in Mr. Lorenzo's favor. Although he would not be permitted to simply transfer the assets from one airline under the umbrella of Texas Air Corporation to another, Federal Bankruptcy Judge Burton R. Lifland ruled that Mr. Lorenzo could *sell* Eastern Airlines' assets to another airline under Texas Air Corporation ownership. His ownership. What followed was the systematic dismantling of the company. All of Eastern's valuable assets, including its ten-million-dollar state of the art reservation system, were sold to Continental Airlines at a significant discount to fair value. All under the guise of strengthening Eastern's cash position. In early February 1991, no longer able to stay afloat, Eastern Airlines officially closed its doors for good.

16. Finishing What He Started

Sometime in June of 1989, in the midst of walking the picket line at Newark Airport and attending union meetings, my father heard about a job that caught his attention. Saudi Arabian Airlines was looking for qualified L-1011 captains for a temporary four-month assignment leading up to the Hajj, the country's annual Islamic pilgrimage to Mecca. To cover the large increase in travel demand the airline needed to put additional planes in the air, but it didn't have enough qualified captains. An American Airlines captain based in Florida was in charge of recruiting the needed Eastern Airlines personnel which included five captains and one flight engineer from the company's Miami base, and one captain, my father, from the New York area.

The Saudis handled their business in the air a bit differently than my dad or any of the other American trained pilots were accustomed to, and they were unbending when it came to their protocols and standard operating procedures. Something as simple as verbal commands within the cockpit between pilots required a very specific verbiage which, while second nature to a Saudi pilot, came with some difficulty to American pilots with decades of experience, who were used to doing it a different way. Ground school and flight training ate up more than two months of the four-month contract. I find that part particularly odd given that these were all seasoned commercial L-1011 captains. Even more surprising was the fact that my father was the only captain to survive the training, the other four having washed out or quit. He describes the training as, "Spartan to say the least," and says he lost twenty to twenty-five pounds in the process. In addition, I'm sure that being so far away from home for an extended period, and missing his family, along with the uncertain future of his beloved Eastern Airlines weighing heavy on his mind, had an impact on his eating and overall health. Also, it's pretty damn hot over there!

Captain Wilbur completed the remainder of his contract with Saudi Arabian Airlines sometime in late September 1989. Despite the difficulties, he'd developed a good rapport with the Saudis and asked their personnel manager, Abdul Aziz Nawar, if he could come back and work for them should things at Eastern go south. Mr. Nawar's response was an unflinching "Yes."

It was back to ALPA meetings, walking the picket line at the upper level of Newark Airport, and more and more bad news regarding his company. In late October 1989, my father fell into conversation with a fellow pilot who had knowledge of an interesting job opportunity. It was suggested that he contact a pilot named Louis DuCapp who worked for a Canadian company called Air Transit. The company had leased an L-1011, which was sitting in a hangar at Hong Kong International Airport. What they needed was a qualified L-1011 captain to accompany Louis' crew to Hong Kong and ferry the plane to Santa Barbara, California, where it would undergo an internal overhaul, and be put into service by the company. Given his recent stint over in Saudi Arabia, my father's flight status was current. That, along with his reputation, got him the job offer over scores of other out-of-work captains who were thirsting to get back in the air. He signed the contract with Air Transit and what followed was a trip around the world, minus about fifteen miles or so.

He and Louis' crew flew as passengers from JFK International Airport to London, England, via British Airways. From there they continued on to Dubai in the United Arab Emirates, and then on to Hong Kong. The guys spent three or four days in Hong Kong checking out the plane and seeing the sites. On November 6, 1989, the crew, with my dad as captain, began their long journey home. They flew to Tokyo, Japan, where they refueled and took on provisions, before taking off on an eight-and-a-half-hour flight to Seattle, Washington. After clearing customs and taking a bit of a rest, the L-1011 refueled for its two-hour flight to Santa Barbara, California. With the contract successfully completed, Captain Wilbur was paid in cash. He wasted little time catching a short flight to LAX, followed by the five-hour flight to Newark International, and home sweet home. Had he flown into JFK he would have officially circumnavigated the globe.

By March of 1990, a full year into the strike, there was no good news on the horizon regarding Eastern. A portion of my father's very last paycheck, which he received in April 1989, went to pay my last college tuition bill. The Airline Pilots Association paid strike benefits in the amount of roughly $200 a week. There were tough decisions ahead for a fifty-six-year old pilot who'd invested thirty years of his life in a company that was now being torn apart. With the liquidation of Eastern Airlines my dad would wind up losing nearly half of his pension. He decided to contact Mr. Nawar and was offered a job as a full-time L-1011 captain for Saudi Arabian Airlines. He did consult my mom before making the phone call and she gave the move her tacit endorsement. Much as she wasn't looking forward to moving halfway across the world to a country which considered her a second-class citizen, she realized that there was really no good alternative. In addition to my father's drive to continue flying, our family simply needed the money. Eastern pilots who took jobs with other domestic carriers lost their stripes and were stripped of all seniority. Captains wound up flying as second officers and with commensurate pay.

Both my sister and I had finished college at this point and were busy enough working on careers of our own. Allison had graduated from Regis College in Weston, Massachusetts, in 1988, and by day was working as a teacher at the Fred S. Keller School in Yonkers, New York. At night she attended classes at Colombia University where she would earn a master's degree in special education with a specialty in applied behavior analysis. I graduated from Fairfield University in Fairfield, Connecticut, in May of 1989, and was working at a small company in Clifton, New Jersey. I went back to school a year later and eventually earned a master's in criminal justice from Rutgers University. Things were stable on the home front, and with his beloved Eastern Airlines slowly dying, and with bills still needing to be paid, my dad accepted Mr. Nawar's job offer.

In late March 1990, my dad flew to the Kingdom of Saudi Arabia where, after a short re-training flight, he began four more years of line flying as a captain on the Lockheed L-1011. He lived in temporary housing until my mom arrived two weeks later, after which they picked out a small third floor walk-up apartment in a very unique place known as Saudia City. Located in the northern part of Jeddah on the west coast of Saudi Arabia, Saudia City is a rectangular walled compound measuring one and a quarter by three quarters of a mile. It was built to house foreign nationals working in various industries within the kingdom.

Jeddah is the largest seaport on the Red Sea, has a population of more than four million people, and is a major gateway for trade for the Middle East, Europe, and the West. In addition to other pilots, there were military personnel, oil workers, teachers, doctors, and other professionals living in the compound. Inside the guarded walls of Saudia City were all the comforts of home including a grocery store, bank, dry cleaner, gas station, a restaurant, a furniture store, tennis courts, swimming pools, and even a movie rental store. Segregating westerners in such a way serves a dual purpose for the Saudis. First, you want to keep your ex-patriot employees happy, and having them live in an environment so similar to their own obviously eases the acclimation process. Second, it has always been my contention that keeping western influence from making a large footprint on its populace is, to the Saudis, a solid ancillary benefit. I believe

169

that they simply don't want their people potentially corrupted by a large and on-going western presence.

Those living in Saudia City, including my parents, were free to venture out. Jeddah is a beautifully vibrant place with a gorgeous beach along the eastern coastline of the Red Sea. The city has a storied history with lots of sites to see. It's clean, crime free, and is, of course, rich with Middle Eastern culture. There are some terrific restaurants and open-air markets in Jeddah where just about everything is for sale. Women were strictly prohibited from leaving the protective walls of the city alone, and they were not allowed to drive. When my father was out on trips, my mom would occasionally go out with other women from the community, and free taxi service was made available for just that purpose. Women were free to dress as they liked within Saudia City, but when they left the compound and mixed with the locals, they were required to adhere to the rules governing Muslim women. Flashy clothes were a no-no, as were exposed hair or skin. My mom bought several abayas and Hawaiian moo-moos for her trips around Jeddah.

Alcohol was, and is, of course, strictly prohibited. How, you might ask, did a group of thirsty non-Muslim pilots, oil workers, and military men, etc., quench their thirst? Small homemade distilleries and kits for brewing beer could be found in several homes and apartments where get togethers took place within the complex. These gatherings added a sense of normalcy and were a great ice breaker for making new friends.

My dad bought a small used car to get back and forth from the airport and for local drives around Jeddah. In his four years with Saudi Arabian Airlines he flew the L-1011 all over Africa, Europe, and the Middle East. Once, during Operation Desert

Shield, he flew a cache of gas masks from Jeddah to Riyadh, Saudi Arabia, for distribution to American and allied forces. He came home only a couple of times a year during that four-year period and my sister and I missed him greatly. My mom came home a lot more often, spending about five months home and seven months with him over seas.

A round trip from Jeddah to Nairobi, Kenya, on March 28, 1994, two days before his sixtieth birthday, was the very last flight of the storied career of Captain Robert M. Wilbur, Jr. Today, he and my mom are alive and well and living in Palm Beach Gardens, Florida. They come up to New Jersey quite often to see Allison and me, as well as their three grandchildren, Allison's two daughters, Amanda and Alissa, and my son, Robert.

Saudia City

17. Reconnecting With The Hartleys

During the course of my research for this book I had the pleasure of speaking with and corresponding with some of Jim Hartley's family. When I asked his daughter, Debra Hartley Perry, about her early childhood and her recollections of her father, she said she was very hurt by her parent's breakup. She remembers that she and her brother James continued to see their father after the divorce, but everything changed when they moved away. Although she was only around eight years old at the time, Debra remembers that neither she nor her brother wanted to leave Florida and move to Hawaii. She described herself as, "Daddy's little girl," and said that for so many years she blocked out memories of her father because they were too painful to recall. The memories would almost always be accompanied by her daydreaming of the terrible pain she would inflict on her father's killer. It caused her a great deal of anxiety, and after a while, she just stopped thinking about him. Debra said that her brother James, only seven years old at the time of the hijacking, very rarely spoke about their father over the years, and claimed to have scant few memories of him. She speculates that he too blocked out memories of their dad. James never married. He lived in Hawaii until his unfortunate passing in 2006 from Multiple Sclerosis.

Debra recently retired from the healthcare industry and still lives in Oahu. She has two daughters, Danila Brown and Gemina Ferreira, and four grandchildren. Gemina, her husband, Kekoa, and their three kids live close by in Oahu. Dani and her husband Josh live in Cheney, Washington with their nine year old daughter Sora. Josh is a veteran air force pilot who has experienced numerous deployments to the Middle East, most recently Afghanistan. As of this writing he flies the Boeing KC-135. Dani and Josh married in 2005, and have lived a typically nomadic military life-style, moving from station to station. They've lived in Grand Forks, North Dakota, Ramstein AFB in Germany, Spokane, Washington and Los Angeles, California, before finally settling in Cheney in 2014.

Dani was always curious about the hero grandfather she never met. Growing up she heard the story of Eastern Airlines Flight 1320 many times, and as the years went by she decided that she just had to know more. While researching the hijacking on the internet in 2004, Dani came across a wonderful article on the subject written for the Silver Falcons, a website/blog dedicated to Eastern Airlines retired pilots and flight attendants. It was a monologue written by my dad's old friend JP Tristani in the year 2000, in honor of the thirtieth anniversary of the hijacking. Dani was able to contact J.P. and the two exchanged information and several emails. As it happened, J.P. was planning to see my parents within the next few weeks, as they were scheduled to come up to New Jersey for a family visit. He told my dad that he'd been contacted by Jim Hartley's granddaughter, a nice young girl named Dani, who really wanted to speak with him.

As uncomfortable as he was, and is, with the subject matter, my dad couldn't bring himself to deny the request, and told J.P. to give Dani his number. When the two spoke over the phone sometime in 2004, Dani had about a million questions about her grandfather. She wanted to know all about how Jim and my dad met, how well they knew each other, and what he was like as a person and a pilot. The two had a nice conversation and my dad has always been glad that he got a chance to speak with her. Quite naturally, Dani had lots of questions about the hijacking, and the role her grandfather played in saving seventy-two lives. Even more than usual, my dad found it difficult to rehash the events of that night. After all, this was no reporter, or some generic stranger asking about the hijacking. It wasn't someone whom he could brush aside with a generic canned answer offering little or no detail. This was Jim Hartley's granddaughter, and she was asking my father, the captain of Eastern Airlines Flight 1320, what exactly happened that resulted in the death of her grandfather. A cursory description of the event just wouldn't suffice, but it was all he had the strength to offer. My mother, who happened to be by his side during the conversation, threw him a much needed lifeline. She had a rather lengthy conversation with Dani and provided her with an account of the specifics of the hijacking in as much detail as she could recall. Dani was very happy to have spoken with my parents, and they satisfied her curiosity to a degree, but her research would continue. When I contacted her in the summer of 2016, she was happy to share information, and was thrilled to learn more about her grandfather. We've had on-going correspondence ever since.

The Hartleys and our family have a shared history based on a singular event which happened nearly fifty years ago. But the hijacking of Eastern Airlines Flight 1320 is so monumental in the annals of aviation history, and the heroism displayed by Jim and my dad was so unbelievable, that the connection between the two families, now re-established, won't soon be broken.

***

Stephen Fowler commented, "It always struck me how quickly the fervor of the event died down...Everyone at Eastern knew about Captain Wilbur and what he'd done, and I think nearly everyone in the industry knew... [It was] a monumental piece of aviation history... Why it wasn't made a bigger deal is a mystery."

The story of the hijacking faded so much more quickly than you might imagine an event of such magnitude ever could. Sure, the era in which it happened certainly had a lot to do with it. Circa 1970 there wasn't a twenty-four-hour news cycle, but it was much more than that. After the initial fervor of the incident, after all the testimonials and ceremonies and awards were handed out, Eastern Airlines wanted the story to go away. It was certainly not good for business. And as for my father, he had absolutely no intention of talking about the experience with anyone, let alone news media. He denied request after request for interviews, and outside of the airline industry, the story of the hijacking of Eastern Airlines Flight 1320 was soon forgotten. Within the industry, however, especially among his fellow Eastern employees, he was treated like royalty.

No doubt, the hijacking was a seminal moment in aviation history, but I think even that description sells it short. The amazing selflessness and bravery displayed by First Officer James E. Hartley, Jr. and Captain Robert M. Wilbur, Jr. demonstrate the very best of what men are capable of. In today's world it's important to be reminded that such valor once existed, and is still a part of the human condition, even if it seems that cowardice and evil so often rule the day.

17. Epilogue

So why write this book now, all these years later? I said at the very beginning of this story that we, as a family, were weaned on silence when it came to the subject of the hijacking. When my sister and I grew older, we would occasionally bring up the idea of commissioning a book in an effort to tell our father's story, but the idea was always met with significant resistance. Over the years all the people who have come into our lives and gotten close enough to hear the story of Eastern Airlines Flight 1320, are aghast by it, and can hardly believe that such an epic event remains virtually unknown to the general public. None of them had ever heard about it before.

We heard time and time again from people we would come to love and respect; close friends, significant others, husbands, and wives, that the story of our father's hijacking absolutely had to be told. While this most certainly had an impact, wearing down a man like my father was no easy task. Not only is he strong willed, self-deprecating, and uncomfortable with the spotlight, there are still lingering feelings of survivor guilt within him, even all these years later. It was an undertaking akin to a slow geological event, like the formation of the Grand Canyon perhaps. And similarly, only a combination of forces played out over a significant period of time would have the strength to break my father down and allow his story to finally come out of the shadows.

When his grandchildren came along and were old enough to hear the story, they, like everyone else, were wide eyed and full of questions. My niece, Amanda, now a recent college graduate, chose her grandfather as the subject of a fifth-grade writing piece:

There's Snow-body Like You

There is snow-body like my grandpa. He taught me how important bravery is. My grandpa is a retired pilot. A long time ago my grandpa was flying an airplane for Eastern Airlines. He had to be very brave. After a while on the plane, someone snuck into the cockpit and told him where to land the plane. My grandpa knew where he had to land, so he ignored the person. The person was a highjacker and he was getting angry. My grandpa refused to land the plane where the highjacker wanted, so the highjacker shot his arm. My grandpa was alright, but the highjacker killed the copilot. My grandpa took the gun and hit him on the head. The highjacker fell unconscious. My grandpa managed to land the plane and saved seventy-three lives. He is my hero and there is snow-body like my grandpa.

Amanda Devine
1/7/08

***

When my son, Robert, was a fifth grader he was tasked with writing a short story based on the, "I Survived," childrens' book series by Lauren Tarshis. The series is meant to educate young readers about some of history's most tragic and deadly events. Books include: *I Survived the Sinking of the Titanic*; *I Survived the Attacks of September 11, 2001*; *I Survived the Great Chicago Fire of 1871*, you get the idea. Tarshis places a fictional character or characters within the setting of the historical event and develops the story around how they survived the ordeal. My son and his classmates had to place themselves in the middle of the fray of such an event and describe how they survived. Robert chose to write about "The Hijacking of Eastern Airlines Flight 1320."

Robert M. Wilbur III

I Survived the Eastern Airlines Hijacking of 1970: Flight 1320 by Robert Wilbur

My name is Robert Wilbur and St. Patrick's Day is one of my favorite holidays because I always visit my aunt, and now I'm on a flight to Boston to see her. "Flight 1320 ready for takeoff" announced the captain. The man sitting next to me was shaking and this was the weird part, he was holding something shiny. I couldn't make it out, but it looked like a police badge. Again, I just stayed in my seat trying to be calm.

At first I thought, this must be a cop trying to protect me, but it was the exact opposite. This guy was acting shifty the whole flight. Every second he asked for a drink, and he kept getting up. After what seemed a long time, I left my seat to go to the bathroom. The flight attendant came around collecting fares. When she got to the strange man, he told her he didn't have any money, but asked to see the captain about it. The flight attendant was about to say no, but then she saw a shiny shiny .38 caliber revolver.

"Right this way sir." The strange man was led to the cockpit. On my way back from the bathroom I ran into them and the man said, "Hey, get outta my way kid." The flight attendant whispered to the captain, "He has a gun." The man said 3 words, "Take me east." In response, the captain said, "We'll be over the ocean and run out of fuel." The hijacker, his name was John Divivo, turned to the co-pilot and shot him in the chest.

Everyone on the plane, including me, started to get freaked out and frightened by the noise. We knew something was wrong from...the firecrackers? Then I knew it was gunfire. Since no one would stand up and do what's right, I ran into the cockpit and threw myself at the hijacker. As he got up, he pointed the gun right at my head. The captain yelled, "Get out of the way, kid."

Just then, he pushed me out of the way making Divivo shoot at nothing. The captain threw Divivo against the side of the plane, knocking him out. The lunatic woke up and grabbed my leg. I couldn't get away! Now controlling the revolver, the captain repeatedly hit Divivo with the butt of the gun rendering him unconscious. With bullet wounds in both arms the captain regained control of the plane landing it in Logan International Airport in Boston, Massachusetts, saving 72 people including himself and me. When we got off the plane he said to me, "You did good kid, you did good."

In the end, co-pilot James E. Hartley died of the gunshot wounds he suffered in the attempted hijacking of Eastern Airlines Flight 1320. Eastern Airline's training center in Miami, Florida was renamed the James E. Hartley Training Center. He is a true hero. While awaiting trial in Boston's Suffolk County Jail, John Divivo hung himself.

As for Captain Robert Wilbur, he is alive and well and just so happens to be my grandfather. I spend quality time with him and will be attending his 80th birthday party in March 2014. My grandfather received many awards and has been interviewed lot of times over the years. He never likes to talk about the details of this tragic event. I'm only 10 years old and was obviously not on Eastern Airlines Flight 1320 on March 17, 1970.

Pressure now being applied by a third generation didn't quite blow the floodgates open, but over time it had the effect of softening my father on the idea, and he eventually relented. I volunteered to take on the project and, although it eventually turned into a labor of love, I realized quickly what an arduous task it would be. Not being a writer by trade, I certainly had my hands full and usually felt somewhat out of my depth. I did my very best and it's my sincerest hope that this book was able to do their story justice.

***

There's a poem I remember hearing many years ago that somehow popped into my head while I was writing this book. I've wracked my brain, but for the life of me I can't recall where, or under what circumstance, I first heard it. I do remember that it moved me a great deal at the time, and still does. It was written by an American pilot named Gill Robb Wilson, a World War I veteran and ordained Presbyterian minister. He was an early editor of *Flying Magazine*, where the poem was likely published prior to his death in 1966. Without a doubt, it describes the essence of what it means to be a pilot better than I ever could.

One of the Trusted
Gill Robb Wilson

You are at cruising altitude.
The westering sun is pink on the disk.
Your eye flicks the gauges. The engines are contented.
Another day another dollar.

You look down at your hands on the wheel.
They are veined and hard and brown.
Tonight you notice they look a little old.
And, by George, they are old. But how can this be?
Only yesterday you were in flying school.
Time is a thief. You have been robbed.
And what have you to show for it?
A pilot, forty years a pilot, a senior pilot.
But what of it, just a pilot.
Then the voice of the stewardess
breaks in on your reverie. The trip is running full,
eighty-four passengers, can she begin
to serve dinner to the passengers?

The passengers, oh yes, the passengers.
You noticed the line of them coming aboard,
the businessmen, the young mothers
with the children in tow, the old couple,
the two priests, the four dogfaces.

A thousand times you have watched them
file aboard and a thousand times disembark.
They always seem a little grayer after the landing
than before the take-off. Beyond doubt
they are always somewhat apprehensive aloft.
But why do they continuously come up here
in the dark sky despite their apprehension?
You have often wondered about that.
You look down at your hands again
and suddenly it comes to you.

They come because they trust you,
you the pilot. They turn over their lives
and their loved ones and their hopes and dreams
to you for safe keeping.
To be a pilot means to be one of the trusted.
They pray in the storm
that you are skillful and strong and wise.
To be a pilot is to hold life in your hands,
to be worthy of faith.

No, you have not been robbed.
You aren't "just a pilot." There is no such thing
as "just a pilot." Your job is a trust.
The years have been a trust.
You have been one of the trusted. Who can be more?

Acknowledgments

This book would not have been possible without the help of long-time family friend and former Eastern Airlines Captain, J.P. Tristani. He helped connect me with some of the people I needed to interview and, whenever possible, steered me in the right direction, enabling me to find others. My mom, Anita Wilbur, dug through mounds of paperwork and pictures in an effort to help piece together my dad's family history. He helped some too, and, additionally, made himself surprisingly available to answer my myriad questions. My sister Allison helped with interviews and it was she who came up with the book's title.

My editor and friend, Susan Vanommeren, added polish to the final manuscript. Her light, yet surehanded touch, pushed it across the finish line, and for that I am grateful. My wife, Patty, served as my number one sounding board and proof reader. She and my son Robert were always gracious enough to allow me priority access to valuable computer time during my nearly four years as an author. Last but not least, a special thanks to Danila (Dani) Brown, Jim Hartley's granddaughter. She was my go-to for information on the Hartley family and her help will always be greatly appreciated.

Bibliography

Aircraft Photographs provided by Google Images: C-119 "Flying Boxcar and C-130 "Hercules", 1-16-16, Martin-404, 2-3-16, Eastern Airlines L-1049C Super Constellation and Cockpit, Lockheed L-188 Electra and Douglas DC-8-21, Boeing 727 and Airbus A-300, 4-4-16, Douglas DC-9, 4-5-16

"Daedalian Civilian Air Safety Award," daedalians.org/.

"Eisenhower Proposes New Middle East Policy." *History.com*. Ed. History.com Staff. A&E Television Networks, n.d. Web. 15 May 2017.

Emerson, Steven, and Brian Duffy. *The Fall of Pan Am 103: Inside the Lockerbie Investigation*. New York, NY: Putnam, 1990. Print.

FBI, Record Management Division- Archives. Investigation of the Hijacking of Eastern Airlines Flight 1320. Accessed via FOIA, April, 2016

"Gill Robb Wilson." *Wikipedia*. Wikimedia Foundation, n.d. Web. 07 May 2016.

Hauser, Christine. "Where Is D.B. Cooper? FBI Ends It's 45 Year Manhunt." *NYTimes.com*. N.p., 13 July 2016. Web. 12 Jan. 2017.

Interview with Arlene Florence Albino, February 13, 2016, Sparta, NJ, June 10, 2016, Long Branch, NJ, June 17, 2016, by telephone.

Interview with Charlotte Williams of Ocean Springs, Ms., January 18, 2017, and January 30, 2017, by telephone.

Interview with Danila Hartley-Brown, July 14, 2016, by telephone. E-mail correspondence on-going.

Interview with Debra Hartley-Perry of Honolulu, Hi., August 1, 2016, August 15, 2016, February 1, 2017, and on-going, by telephone.

Interviews with Eastern Airlines Flight 1320 Captain Robert M. Wilbur, Jr., November 4, 2015-February 18, 2018, in person and by telephone at various locations.

Interviews with Eastern Airlines Flight 1320 passenger Emanuel Abrams, March 20, 2016, Newton, Mass, and October 26, 2016, by telephone.

Interview with Eastern Airlines Flight 1320 passenger Peggy McLoughlin, March 20, 2016, Newton, Mass, and October 21, 2016, and November 22, 2016, by telephone.

Interview with former Eastern Airlines employee Steve Fowler of Yuma, Az, August 29, 2016, and February 16, 2017, by telephone.

Interview with Louis B. Peterson, Graham, Wa., August 19, 2016, by telephone.

Interview with Marjorie Braun of Phoenix, Az, December 8, 2017 and December 20, 2016, by telephone.

Interview with Mary Kirwan of Buffalo, NY, October 17, 2016, by telephone

Interview with Retired E.A.L. Captain James Hamilton, March 22, 2017, Neptune, NJ., and March 26, 2017 by telephone.

Interview with Retired E.A.L. Captain Murray E. Burke (Buddy) of Montvale, NJ., February 19, 2017, by telephone.

Interview with Sandra Kay Saltzer, June 24, 2016, Shortsville, NY, and July 1, 2016, by telephone.

Interview with Vernon E. Peterson, August 1, 2016, Hawthorn, NJ.

Jane Engle | Los Angeles Times Staff Writer. "U.S. Aviation Security Timeline." *Los Angeles Times*. Los Angeles Times, 12 June 2011. Web. 09 Feb. 2016.

J.P. Tristani. "Death In The Sky…Hopes For The Future, Eastern Airlines Flight 1320, March 17, 1970". May 6, 2000.

"Martha Raye." Wikipedia, Wikipedia Foundation, 28 July 2018, en.wikipedia.org/wiki/Martha_Raye.

McCabe, Scott. "Crime History, Oct. 29, 1972: Suburban D.C. Bank Robbers Hijack Plane to Cuba - D.C. Crime Stories." *DC Crime Stories*. N.p., 29 Oct. 2013. Web. 26 July 2016.

"National Academy." *FBI*. FBI, 30 Nov. 2015. Web. 12 Sept. 2016.

"Off With Your Shoes, A brief History of Airport Security". N.p., n.d. Web. 12 Feb 2016

"Rasheed Air Base." *Wikipedia*. Wikimedia Foundation, 30 Apr. 2017. Web. 15 May 2017.

Salpukas, Agis. "EASTERN'S BOARD AGREES TO TAKEOVER BY TEXAS AIR." *The New York Times*, The New York Times, 24 Feb. 1986, www.nytimes.com/1986/02/25/business/eastern-s-board-agrees-to-takeover-by-texas-air.html?mcubz=1

"Texas Air Corporation." *Wikipedia*, Wikimedia Foundation, 7 Oct. 2017, en.wikipedia.org/wiki/Texas_Air_Corporation.

"The 1974 Air Transportation Security Act." <i>Wikipedia</i>. Wikimedia Foundation, n.d. Web. 09 Feb. 2016.

"The Hijacking of Flight 1320 and The Heroism of Captain Bob Wilbur and First Officer James Hartley." <i>The REAL Word, The Official Newsletter of the Silver Falcons</i> 18.4 (Fall, 2014): 4-5. Web.

"USATODAY.com - Timeline of Airline Security Measures." <i>USATODAY.com - Timeline of Airline Security Measures</i>. N.p., 17 Sept. 2001. Web. 09 Feb. 2016.

Pictures and More

Mrs. Eugene L. Bishop Jr.
2220 Pinecrest Road
Greensboro, North Carolina 27403

Dear Capt. Wilbur,

My husband was a passenger on the shuttle flight that became such a tragedy. Every day I think of you, your co-pilot & your families. I try to think of words to say what is in my heart, & I am blank. Words are not enough. Nothing is, nor ever will be. Fourteen years ago, in El Paso, my 3 year old son & 5 year old daughter, watched a plane go down, burning. The pilot chose to stay with his plane & take it away from the city. He died, ofcourse. He could have saved his life, but would have let his plane crash on a school yard. I think his name was Capt Anderson, stationed at Biggs AFB, but it has been a long time, & names slip away. Still, we remember him, as do many others, still in El Paso. To us, he was a hero in every respect, & we all gained something deep inside, just being where it happened. This may not make a lot of since to you, but that is only because I am not good with words.

You & Mrs. Hartley fall into that same category. I sincerely grieve for Mr Hartley. America needs men like him. And you. We are all fortunate that you still live. Our prayers now are that your injuries heal entirely.

You are, in every respect, a hero. You will probably not receive awards, riches, or fame. But you are a HERO. And you will remain in our hearts forever. Had it not been for you, my husband would not have called me this evening, or the evening before, or the evening before that. Had it not been for you, I would be a widow & 6 children would have been fatherless. But this is just one family. There were 69 others aboard. Nothing any of us can say or do can repay. All we can do is to remember. Small consolation for Mrs. Hartley, & little comfort to you in your present condition. But I must write to you. I must be sure you know we care. I feel a terrible guilt, because of the horrible inadequacy of a letter, but I know not what to do. How can I ever say "Thanks" for keeping my husband safe?

I pray your wounds heal well, & that your life, once more, is good. And I hope the knowledge that we are your friends, gives you some comfort. Although we will probably never meet, we'll always be your friend. And we'll remember.

God Bless.

Sincerely,
Norma Bishop

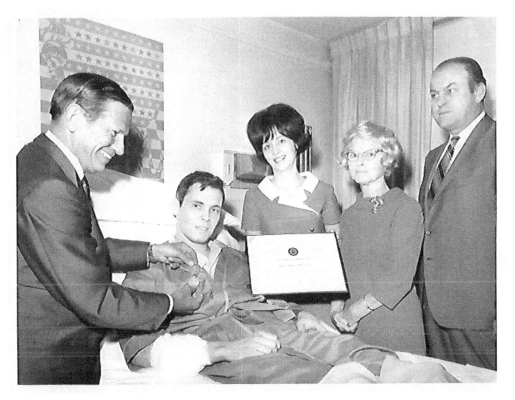

Captain Robert Wilbur recovering at Massachusetts General Hospital

Robert and Charlotte 1941

Bob Wilbur Sr. with Elsie

Charlotte, Elsie (Mom), and Robert

Robert at Riverside Academy

Robert in the United States Air Force

Air Force Days

Reluctant Hero

EASTERN AIR LINES
INCORPORATED
MEMBER OF THE NATIONAL SAFETY COUNCIL
MIAMI INTERNATIONAL AIRPORT
MIAMI 48, FLORIDA

Mr. Robert M. Wilbur, Jr.
Woodside Drive
Plant City, Fla.

July 21, 1959

Dear Sir:

This is in reference to your application for a position as copilot. In order that you may be given further consideration for possible employment, it will be necessary for you to report to our Employment Office, 4500 N. W. 36th St., Miami, Fla. for an interview and to complete certain pre-employment tests, the successful completion of which are pre-requisites for employment. <u>You should complete the enclosed duplicate application and take it with you</u> to aid our Personnel Representative in his interview. Also, take the original, a photostat, or a certified copy of your military discharge, pilot's licenses, and log book.

We would appreciate your reporting at 8:00 A.M. on *
By copy of this letter, our Tampa, Fla. Station Manager is authorized to issue you upon request a round trip, space available pass for this purpose. Please remember we cannot authorize transportation on another carrier, and all other expenses incurred on this trip must be borne by you. If you find it impossible to keep this appointment, please advise this office by return mail, suggesting a date you will be able to report. Our offices are open Monday through Friday. After you have completed our personnel processing, your file will be forwarded to my attention, and we will be in a position then to advise you further regarding the possibility of employment.

Members of the Air Transport Association have an agreement whereby they do not consider, or accept for copilot employment, pilots who are currently employed by other scheduled air carriers. When you accept this appointment, we understand you are not so employed. We will expect you to advise us should you accept copilot employment with another scheduled air carrier while your application is being considered for a copilot position with Eastern Air Lines.

Thank you for the interest you have shown in wishing to become associated with Eastern Air Lines. *Please report on a day convenient to you. Capt. Seymour is on vacation and will not be able to interview you. However, if you will complete this preliminary processing, he will be in a better position to advise you regarding your possibilities for future employment when he does return and has an opportunity to review your file. You should make every effort to have your military cards converted

Very truly yours,

EASTERN AIR LINES, INC.

R. R. Seymour

RRS:c to FAA commercial & instrument ratings and apply for your FCC radio license.
enclosure

THERE'S NO SUBSTITUTE FOR EASTERN'S EXPERIENCE

Robert and Anita 1964 (top) and 1965 (bottom)

Anita and Robert holding the Daedalian Civilian Air Safety Award Trophy

Captain Wilbur with George H.W. Bush and Unknown Diplomate Aboard U.N. Flight

Reluctant Hero

PRESIDENT
AND CHIEF EXECUTIVE OFFICER

April 9, 1970

Captain Robert M. Wilbur, Jr.
39-20 Berdan Avenue
Fairlawn, New Jersey 07410

Dear Captain Wilbur:

    It gives me great pleasure to present you with the enclosed Hornet mug on behalf of the employees of Scripto, Inc.

    Mr. Arthur L. Harris, President of Scripto, wrote to me telling me that this mug is one of the last remaining Hornet mugs, which were given by President Nixon to the astronauts on the occasion of the Apollo XI flight. These mugs were produced in Scripto's Florence Ceramics plant in Pasadena, California, and they felt that no one would be more deserving to receive it than you.

    All of us are very pleased that you are recovering so rapidly.

Sincerely,

F. D. Hall

EDWARD J. SULLIVAN
CLERK

COMMONWEALTH OF MASSACHUSETTS
COUNTY OF MIDDLESEX
OFFICE OF CLERK OF THE COURTS

March 20, 1970

Capt. Robert Wilbur
Massachusetts General Hospital
Fruit Street
Boston, Massachusetts 02114

Dear Captain Wilbur,

    Your heroic action in subduing the would-be hijacker of your plane and the subsequent landing under extreme difficulty and danger is to be highly commended.

    Please accept the heartfelt condolences of the citizens of this area at the tragic loss of your co-pilot.

    We, of Middlesex County, wish you speedy recovery, and we trust you, before leaving our state, will realize that the entire nation appreciates what you have done.

                              Yours truly,

                              Edward J. Sullivan
                              Clerk

EJS:mao

617 • 482-0044
CABLE: TRIBALLOVE
TELEX. 94514

March 30, 1970

Captain Robert Wilbur, Jr.
Massachusetts General Hospital
Cambridge Street
Boston, Massachusetts

Dear Captain:

    The entire cast, crew, musicians and staff of HAIR would be greatly honored if you will be our guest at the 6:00 p.m. performance on the first Saturday evening you are free to come and see our production.

    After the performance, we would like you and Mrs. Wilbur to come back stage to join us for dinner. Because of the two performances Saturday evening, we are serving dinner at the theatre and would like so very much if you would be our guest.

    With great admiration I remain sincerely,

Horace Greeley McNab

HGM/dcp

HONORING

TEN GREAT MEN

of Bergen County

Father's Day June 1970

Reluctant Hero

DAY, JUNE 21, 1970

BOWIE K. KUHN -- A father who made the choice of switching careers to provide an inspirational influence on the lives of his children. Attorney, Commissioner of Baseball; active in baseball legal matters since shortly after his graduation from Virginia Law School. Born in Takoma Park, Maryland, a suburb of Washington, D.C. Spent his youth idolizing the Washington Senators. Kuhn is a jogger, golfer, tennis player, and loves books and opera. He enjoys gardening, especially raising roses. Mr. and Mrs. Kuhn have three sons and one daughter. The family dates back in American history. Robert Bowie, his great great grandfather, was Governor of Maryland during the War of 1812 and a great, great uncle, Joseph Kent, also was a former Maryland chief executive and U.S. Senator. Bowie Kuhn is 1970 Fund Drive Chairman, Girl Scout Council of Bergen County.

JOHN J. LATTANZIO -- For 15 years a leader in Boys Club affairs. Helped acquire 50-acre camp near Hyde Park, N.Y., and large financial grants to make Lodi Boys Club one of the outstanding in the East. First recipient of the Boys Club Lifeline Award; earned National Boys Club Award; served as State Chairman, local President. Member, Bergen County Welfare Board. Mr. and Mrs. Lattanzio have two daughters, both school teachers.

LIEUTENANT-COLONEL WALLACE W. PRICE (Ret.) -- Served in the Army for 21 years, advancing through the ranks. President, Urban League for Bergen County; First Vice Chairman, Bergen County United Fund, President, Business and Professional Men's Opportunities, Inc., New York; member, Advisory Board for Community Relations, Teaneck; co-founder, EDGES, a regional group of business personnel assisting in securing higher level positions for blacks; member, Defense Supply Association, West Point Chapter, and is Associate to the Special Director, Legal Defense and Educational Fund, N.Y. Colonel Price is Manager of Procedures, Financial and Administration Departments, Olin Corporation, Stamford, Conn. Holds bachelor's degree in Education from Southern Illinois University; M.S. in Guidance, magna cum laude, Virginia State College; and has done post graduate work at University of Pennsylvania. Colonel and Mrs. Price, Teaneck residents since 1964, have three children aged 18, 13, and 10.

EARL UBELL -- An extraordinary blend of scientific and humanistic values. His concept of the contribution of aesthetics to enjoyment of life has opened cultural vistas to young and old in all walks of life. President, North Jersey Cultural Council; Chairman, Board of the Center for Modern Dance Education; Chairman, Arts Committee, Bergen County Y.M.H.A.; Advisory Committee, United Fund. Holder of B.S. degree from City College in New York, Mr. Ubell is interested in writing, mathematics and dancing. A native of Brooklyn, he has been a Hackensack resident for 10 years; of Bergen for 17 years. Mr. and Mrs. Ubell have two children, a daughter Lori, 18; and a son, Michael, 17. He is science editor of WCBS-TV.

ROBERT M. WILBUR JR. -- A hero of our times. He is the Eastern Airlines pilot who, shot in both arms, in March, landed safely a hijacked airliner with 73 persons aboard in Boston, after a cockpit struggle with the would-be hijacker. Born in Lakeland, Florida, Captain Wilbur has been a Fair Lawn resident for three years. He attended Riverside Military Academy and the University of Florida. He enjoys sports of all kinds. Captain and Mrs. Wilbur have two children, Allison Marie, 4; and Robert Milton III, 2.

Our young family after the hijacking, Allison, Anita, Robert Jr. , Robert III

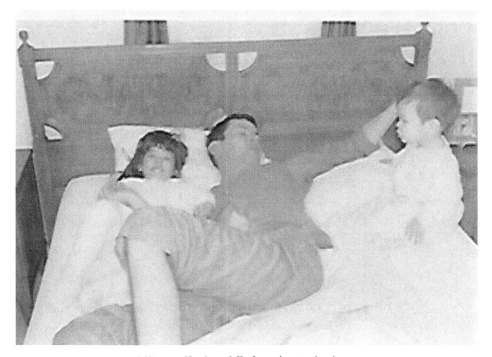

Allison, Dad and Robert just relaxing.

Allison and Rob

Captain Robert M. Wilbur, Jr. at sunset circa mid 1970s.

Captain Robert M. Wilbur, Jr 1993

First Officer James E. Hartley Jr.

Teenage Jim Hartley Jr.

UNITED STATES ARMED FORCES
CONSENT, DECLARATION OF PARENT OR LEGAL GUARDIAN
(FOR THE ENLISTMENT OF A MINOR IN THE U.S. ARMED FORCES)

LAST NAME – FIRST NAME – MIDDLE NAME OF APPLICANT FOR ENLISTMENT	DATE		
	DAY	MONTH	YEAR
HARTLEY, JAMES EDWARD JR.	4	April	1957

PLACE OF APPLICATION FOR ENLISTMENT	SERVICE OR COMPONENT FOR WHICH CONSENT IS GIVEN
Miami, Florida	U. S. Army

NAME OF PARENT(S) OR LEGAL GUARDIAN SIGNING CONSENT	RELATIONSHIP (Father, Mother, Legal Guardian)
James Edward Hartley, Sr. & Sadie Dobbs Hartley	Father & Mother

ADDRESS (Number and street or RFD, City or Town)	COUNTY	STATE

ADDRESS OF OTHER PARENT IF SEPARATED (Number and street or RFD, City or Town)	COUNTY	STATE

PLACE OF BIRTH OF APPLICANT (City or Town and State)	DATE OF BIRTH		
	DAY	MONTH	YEAR
Jacksonville, Florida	15	November	1939

I/WE DO HEREBY CERTIFY, THAT THE ABOVE APPLICANT HAS NO OTHER LEGAL GUARDIAN THAN ME/US, AND I/WE HEREBY CONSENT TO HIS/HER ENLISTMENT IN THE SERVICE OR COMPONENT OF THE ARMED FORCES AS INDICATED ABOVE, SUBJECT TO ALL THE REQUIREMENTS AND LAWFUL COMMANDS OF THE OFFICERS WHO MAY, FROM TIME TO TIME, BE PLACED OVER HIM/HER; AND I/WE HEREBY CERTIFY THAT NO PROMISE OF ANY KIND HAS BEEN MADE TO ME/US CONCERNING ASSIGNMENT TO DUTY OR PROMOTION DURING HIS/HER ENLISTMENT AS AN INDUCEMENT TO ME/US TO SIGN THIS CONSENT; AND I/WE DO HEREBY RELINQUISH ALL CLAIM TO HIS/HER SERVICE AND TO ANY WAGES OR COMPENSATION FOR SUCH SERVICE. (This does not apply to peacetime reserve components) I/WE UNDERSTAND THAT IF HE/SHE BECOMES A CANDIDATE FOR ANY SERVICE ACADEMY, FOR OFFICER CANDIDATE TRAINING OR AVIATION CADET TRAINING AND IF AS A CONSEQUENCE IS REMOVED FROM GENERAL SERVICE IN ORDER TO PREPARE FOR ENTRANCE AND SUBSEQUENTLY FAILS TO PASS THE ENTRANCE EXAMINATIONS, HE/SHE WILL BE RETURNED TO GENERAL SERVICE.

I/WE THOROUGHLY UNDERSTAND THAT I/WE HAVE CONSENTED TO HIS/HER ENLISTMENT IN THE SERVICE OR COMPONENT OF THE U.S. ARMED FORCES INDICATED ABOVE FOR THE PERIOD OF three (3) years.

SIGNATURES OF:

Julian E Tudor Jr — WITNESSING OFFICIAL

James E. Hartley Sr — PARENT OR LEGAL GUARDIAN

RECRUITING OFFICER OR RECRUITER — OTHER PARENT (If required)

VERIFICATION OF DATE AND PLACE OF BIRTH OF APPLICANT (For use by recruiting office)

LAST NAME – FIRST NAME – MIDDLE NAME	PLACE OF BIRTH (City or Town and State)	DATE OF BIRTH		
		DAY	MONTH	YEAR
HARTLEY, JAMES EDWARD	Jacksonville, Florida	15	November	1939

HOW VERIFIED: Birth verified by telegraphic message from Bureau of Vital Statistics, Jacksonville, Fla.

REMARKS:

"The parents and/or guardian have been advised and understand that the enlistee can be assigned to any area or station of service, in the United States or overseas, or any type of duty, authorized by current law and regulations, immediately upon completion of required period of basic training."

Julian E Tudor Jr — SIGNATURE OF RECRUITER

DD FORM 373
1 AUG 50

Jim Hartley Jr. and Shirley Abrahano

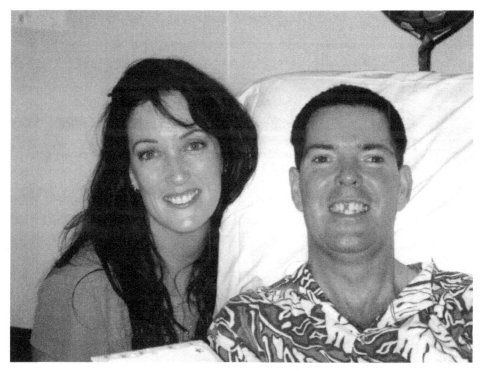

Deborah and James E. Hartley III (Jim's daughter and son)

Teenage Jim Hartley III circa 1991

Joshua, Dani (Jim's Granddaughter) and Daughter Sori 2016

Christine, Sandy and Arlene receive their Award.

Sandra K. Saltzer in her Eastern Airlines uniform.

A young Peggy McLoughlin (passenger)

Barbara and Manny Abrams (passenger)

Bob and Anita New Years Eve 2001

From left to right - Marc Devine, Allison Wilbur Devine, Captain Robert and Anita Wilbur Jr., Patricia Wilbur, Robert Wilbur III, Fall 2001

Aunt Charlotte's family
From left to right Charlotte Williams (nee Wilbur), Dr. Gene Williams, Patsy, Linda, David, Jonathan, James, Sarah, Laura, Christina, Timothy, Rebekah, and Ricky (Holding a picture of Joseph)

Bob and Anita, Spring 2015

Anita and Bob with grandchildren, Alissa, Robert and Amanda 2010

Grandaughters, Amanda and Alissa 2000

2019

Grandson, Robert 2005, Future pilot?

2019

Captain Robert Wilbur Jr., Anita, Allison and Rob 2016

Amanda and Alissa with their grandfather 2018

Allison with fiancé Mike Benton in Italy 2019

Three generations of the Wilbur family
2016

Eastern Airlines Retirees Association Hall of Fame Induction 2016

Dad at Jim Hartley Jr.'s grave, Miami 2017

Made in the USA
Middletown, DE
16 June 2020

98063796R00130